PUFFIN BOOKS

THE PUFFIN BOOK

Television and films have brou[...]
of dance to a very wide audien[...] *[...]in Book of Dance* sets out to
describe clearly the whole world of dance and give each different style
its place.

The scene is set with an outline of the development of ballet from its
origins in the courts of sixteenth-century Italy. Then follows the development of modern dance in the twentieth century as a reaction
against the formality of ballet. The appearance and great popularity of
different forms of dance on screen and in the stage musical are also
described. A useful time chart relates the development of dance to
world events. Life for professional dancers today, whether in ballet,
musicals or television, is challenging. The author describes the sort of
training dancers receive in ballet or theatre schools (such as New York's
School for the Performing Arts or the Royal Ballet School) and then how
they find work and maintain a daily routine.

Dance classes are immensely important even for the working dancer
and the author looks at how classes for ballet, modern dance, jazz and
tap are run. Creating a dance involves a number of people – the
choreographer, the musicians, the notator, the designer and of course
the dancers – and their roles in the process are described. Finally, a
'Who's Who' lists the most famous names in dance and briefly outlines
the importance of each. And a glossary explains many technical terms.

This comprehensive and very readable book is the ideal introduction
to those just developing an interest in the exciting world of dance, as
well as being a useful companion for budding dancers who are already
taking classes.

Craig Dodd has written for many publications including the *Guardian*
and the *Dancing Times*. He has written thirteen books on all types of
dance. He lives in London.

THE PUFFIN BOOK OF
Dance

Craig Dodd

PUFFIN BOOKS

PUFFIN BOOKS

Published by the Penguin Group
27 Wrights Lane, London W8 5TZ, England
Viking Penguin Inc., 40 West 23rd Street, New York, New York 10010, USA
Penguin Books Australia Ltd, Ringwood, Victoria, Australia
Penguin Books Canada Ltd, 2801 John Street, Markham, Ontario, Canada L3R 1B4
Penguin Books (NZ) Ltd, 182–190 Wairau Road, Auckland 10, New Zealand

First published 1989

1 3 5 7 9 10 8 6 4 2

Copyright © Craig Dodd, 1989
Illustrations copyright © G. J. Galsworthy, 1989
All rights reserved

Filmset in 10/12 Linotron Palatino by
Rowland Phototypesetting Ltd, Bury St Edmunds, Suffolk
Made and printed in Great Britain by
Cox and Wyman Ltd, Reading, Berks.

Except in the United States of America, this book is sold subject
to the condition that it shall not, by way of trade or otherwise, be lent,
re-sold, hired out, or otherwise circulated without the publisher's
prior consent in any form of binding or cover other than that in which
it is published and without a similar condition including this condition
being imposed on the subsequent purchaser

■ CONTENTS

INTRODUCTION
Everybody's Doing It

People have always danced, but it is doubtful if they have ever danced as much as they do today. Or if they have ever watched as much dancing as they do today.

There are dances you can do that do not take a lot of skill. There are others you can sit and watch which will have taken years of hard training and constant practice every day to master.

Today dance is always for enjoyment of one sort or another, whether you are doing it or watching it. But this was not always the case.

Long before people thought of dancing for fun or of sitting in a theatre to watch a performance, dance played a more serious part in people's lives. It was an important part of religious ceremonies.

These were not the religions we know today, when people gather to worship Christ or Muhammad. Many were pagan religions and many came from the East. Cave paintings from prehistoric times show people dancing. Egyptian tomb paintings show people dancing. People dance in the decorations on ancient Greek pottery. And we know that some of the last people to be affected by civilization, for example the Australian aborigines, used dance to pray for rain, to ask their gods for victory in the hunt or in war. And afterwards they would dance to thank the gods if they had been lucky.

Some of the earliest forms of dancing that you can still see more or less as they were always danced are

Maori dancers from New Zealand.

performed by the Indians of North America and by the Maoris of New Zealand.

All of this is far away from the world of ballet and disco dancing, but both these dance forms, like all the others, grew out of the dances our ancestors did. Some types of dances changed into those people did for personal enjoyment. Other types changed into those done by trained dancers, often professional.

In the East dancing was an important part of everyday life, although in countries such as Thailand ordinary members of the population were often not allowed to see the most sacred temple dances. The dancers were regarded as almost as holy as the priests and they devoted their whole life to learning their dances and then passing them on to younger dancers. This way many dances have been carefully preserved in their original form for thousands of years.

In the south of India the Kathakali dances are a whole way of life. The dance troupe is made up only of men and boys led by their teacher, known as a guru. They live together as a troupe and make the preparations for the dance – the putting on of the complicated, colourful make-up, costumes and masks – into a solemn ritual. Even the meal they eat before the performance is part of the ritual. The stories of gods and demons which they tell in their dances were a way of passing on religious knowledge to the villagers.

In Japan, dancing was very stylized. The earliest form was called Bugaku and, like early ballet, was only performed for the privileged audiences at the court. The general public were not allowed to see it until after 1945, twelve centuries after it was first performed! Noh plays, which are dance dramas with a lot of mime, developed in the fifteenth century when the samurai (warrior) class became important. The more famous Kabuki theatre has more dancing in it, but the performances were often outrageous, so outrageous that the Japanese rulers banned them. To get around the ban the producers used men to dance the women's parts, a tradition that has continued ever since.

This type of Japanese dance was developing at the same time as ballet in Europe in the sixteenth century.

▓ LET THE PEOPLE DANCE

Folk dances around the world are remarkably similar, even though in the early years when they were developing there was not much communication between countries.

A whole village or tribe or sect would come together to celebrate or enjoy themselves. But enjoying themselves was usually connected to some event, like celebrating a good harvest. The high jumps in English morris dancing were intended to make the corn grow high. Bacchic dances in Ancient Greece were performed to celebrate a particularly good crop of grapes, Bacchus being the god of wine.

Out of these early dances grew what we call folk dances, reflecting everything from the weather to the character of the people.

In Georgia, now part of the Soviet Union, the fiery cossacks do exciting dances with the men, wearing soft leather boots, standing on their toes. The women do flowing dances in which they wave handkerchiefs. In Hungary and other central European countries the czardas and the mazurka developed, reflecting the fiery character of these nations.

Then, as society became more sophisticated, these dances slowly changed. What had been a boisterous folk dance developed into a more polite version, to be performed in the ballroom. The polka from Bohemia was a sensation when introduced into Britain, and it brought quite a lot of criticism with it, as the dancers had to hold each other very tightly in order to swirl around the dance floor.

As ballroom dances became more formal they were in their turn danced by professional ballroom dancers who made the steps look very different from those which had been danced for simple pleasure.

And while folk dances were becoming social dances in this way, the formal dances of the courts of Italy and France were slowly evolving into classical ballet. When ballet reached a peak at the end of the nineteenth century, people wanted change. They did not like the formal style and wanted to free dance from some of the restrictions of the classical style. And so a new dance form evolved – modern dance.

■ THE DANCE EXPLOSION

The dance explosion started at the beginning of this century with new ideas in classical ballet and modern dance. At the same time new social dances were being introduced, particularly in America. It was from there that most new ideas came, introducing many dances from South America as well as those invented by the blacks of North America. These were polished up into stage dances and soon appeared on the Broadway stages in New York.

The coming of talking pictures in 1929 also helped the

spread of dance. Very soon after its invention, musical films were being made, and as early as 1931 Fred Astaire and Ginger Rogers had tap-danced their way across the screen. Busby Berkeley created his fantastic dance patterns using hundreds of dancers, sometimes filmed from above, so that they looked like flowers opening and closing.

In the following years popular dances grew more energetic, with Bop becoming Rock and Roll and reaching a high point with disco dance. The film *Saturday Night Fever* brought a new excitement and interest to the world of dance and everybody has been doing it since. Some have taken it a step further, with dances such as breakdancing, which are often beyond the talents of many.

In the last thirty years exciting Russian dancers have brought new life to ballet in the West and a whole new young audience discovered modern dance. Ballroom dancing has become a great industry, also attracting young people, particularly to formation dance teams. In the theatre, musicals are once again fashionable, with shows like *Cats*, *42nd Street* and *Starlight Express* giving opportunities for dancers to perform and audiences to enjoy.

And dance has influenced other areas as well, not least in sports such as skating. Ice skating discovered dance in the 1950s. Although the Olympic skater Sonja Henie had made musical films involving skating sequences, it was not until the Protopovs first won the World Pair Skating Championships that ballet had any serious effect. Until this time skating had been a purely athletic affair, but these two Russians took the advice of ballet teachers and introduced good line, ballet lifts and a more poetic feeling into their routines.

At this time ice dancing was like ballroom dancing on skates, and the free programmes, which today are so exciting, were then not very different from the present set routines. Men's skating remained solidly athletic.

And then Britain's John Curry started to introduce ballet steps into his routines and also tried to achieve some balletic elegance on the ice. Slowly his ideas became more acceptable and in 1976 he won an Olympic gold medal. More importantly a whole generation of young skaters was influenced by him, including ice dancers.

John Curry on ice.

And soon ice dancing, which was the last skating event to be introduced into the Olympics, became the most popular. Britain had dominated the championships early on. But soon things changed and routines became more theatrical and eventually reached a peak in the early 1980s with the British pair Jane Torvill and Christopher Dean, who made inventive programmes from musicals such as *Mack and Mabel* and *Barnum*, finally achieving perfect sixes for their dramatic dance to Ravel's *Bolero*.

Through their performances yet more people were attracted to the wonderful world of dance.

This book sets out to give you a picture of the world of the professional dancer, concentrating on the sort of dancing which has to be learned seriously, just like any other subject. It will explain how dance started and developed over the years and how it has changed with the times. It will explain how a young dancer can take the first steps to a career in dance at a ballet or theatre school. It will take you behind the scenes of a dance company and introduce you to the world of the choreographer, who makes the dances, the dancer, who performs them, and the notator, who writes them down. It will introduce you to the work of the costume designers, the composers and many other people who take part in the making of a theatrical performance. Technical terms are explained to make it easier for you to understand a performance and there are biographies of many personalities who have been successful in the world of dance.

Dance is a very demanding profession for young dancers, but they all enjoy it, as it is what they have always *wanted* to do. If you want to dance, but don't want to make it your career, the training can be helpful in many ways. And you can always enjoy the fun of the disco at the same time.

FROM THE BEGINNING
Ballet, Modern Dance and Dance on Stage and Screen

■ THE STORY OF BALLET

The oldest ballet still danced regularly is *The Whims of Cupid and the Ballet Master*. It has been performed by the Royal Danish Ballet in Copenhagen ever since 1786, but if the audiences of that day were spirited into 1988 to see the ballet, they probably would not recognize it. The style of dancing has changed so much: dancers now do things which they could not have done in the eighteenth century.

But if the eighteenth-century audience had been taken back in time to the beginnings of ballet, they would have been just as surprised by how far dancing had progressed since the first steps were taken in the small courts of Italy in the fifteenth century.

Classical ballet has its roots in the lavish entertainments which were put on by travelling dancing masters for Italian princes and, later, French kings and queens.

The monarchs and their guests watched from a platform as hundreds of masked and costumed courtiers walked in complicated patterns around the floor. It was not only courtiers who performed for their sovereigns: sometimes the dancing master used acrobats and mimes as well as horsemen, soldiers, dogs and other, more exotic, animals.

As time went by these court entertainments became more and more elaborate. They were used to impress visiting royalty or ambassadors. Food would be wheeled in on great carriages on which people dressed to suit the dish – mermaids and Neptune for the fish course, for example – would perform. For outdoor performances artificial lakes were made, on which model ships would sail. Sometimes the lakes burst their banks, flooding audiences. Wild animals were occasionally used, sometimes with equally dangerous results: once a tiger escaped.

Performances were lit by hundreds of candles and torches, which could start fires in the cramped spaces. In France, one night, when King Charles VI and his friends were making mischief while dressed as apes, the king's brother held out a torch to see them more clearly. The king's costume started to burn and he was only saved because the lady he was with used her heavy skirts to put out the flames!

The most famous of these lavish court entertainments was the *Ballet Comique de la Reine*, which Catherine de Medici, Queen of France, arranged in 1581 to celebrate a royal wedding. It started at ten at night and was still going on at four the following morning. It was devised by the queen's dancing master, Baldassarino di Belgiojoso, whom she had brought with her from Italy. In France, he became known as Balthasar de Beaujoyeux.

Catherine used these entertainments to keep her sons' minds off politics, so that she could run the country when, after her husband's death, all three in turn became Kings of France. By the time Louis XIV came to the throne in 1643 court dancing had become less important. Louis – who was to become known as the Sun King, after his role in the *Ballet de la Nuit* (*The Ballet of the Night*) – revived it.

He enjoyed court entertainments and liked nothing better than to appear in them himself, in the main role, such as Apollo or the Sun, naturally. One of his entertainments, *Les Plaisirs de l'Ile Enchantée* (*The Pleasures of the Enchanted Island*), staged in 1664 at Versailles, lasted for three days. It ended with one of the most dazzling firework displays ever seen in France.

By the end of the 1660s Louis was becoming too old to perform and retired from the dance floor. As a result, the courtiers were forced to stop dancing as well. This meant that professional dancers were needed to entertain them

In 1661 Louis had established L'Académie Royal de la Danse in Paris. He wanted it to bring together the different teaching methods and styles of the time. Its director was Pierre Beauchamp and it was he who first wrote down the five basic positions for the feet which are still the cornerstone of ballet today.

At this time, one of Louis's favourite musicians and composers was the Italian, Jean-Baptiste Lully, who had started his career as a court dancer. In 1669 Louis founded the Paris Opéra: two years later it became L'Académie Royale de Musique and Lully became the most important person there staging operas which usually contained ballet scenes. (This began the tradition which continues to this day, of ballet being performed at the Opéra.)

At first all the dancers were men, but Lully gradually started to use ladies from the court, in parts that had been previously danced by boys. In 1681 the first professional female dancers, led by the beautiful Mademoiselle Lafontaine, made their debut at the Opéra in *La Triomphe de l'Amour* (*The Triumph of Love*). And so Mlle Lafontaine has gone down in history as the first recorded prima ballerina.

Lully wrote more than thirty opera ballets. One night in 1687 when he was conducting one of them, he cut his

A scene from The Triumph of Love, *first performed by the French Court in January 1681 and at the Paris Opéra by professional dancers in May of the same year. Dances were arranged by Beauchamps to music by Lully.*

foot with the stick he used to beat time on the ground: the wound became infected and he died.

At the beginning of the eighteenth century, female dancers were restricted in their movements by their stiff bodices and full court skirts with heavy panniers sticking out at the sides. Often wearing masks, they could do little more than walk elegantly and make little jumps as they moved across the dance floor. The men wore tunics and tights with stiff, short skirts called *tonnelets*, which look a little like the tutus ballerinas wear today. With more freedom to move, male dancers could perform more exciting steps and jumps than the ladies.

Even with these restrictions, by the beginning of the eighteenth century ballet had entered the age of professional dancers, both male and female, who were properly schooled in the traditions of dance and the correct way to perform steps. In 1713, a ballet school was established as part of the Paris Opéra. Its job was to train dancers for the Opéra ballet.

The Rise of the Ballerina

At the start of the eighteenth century, the greatest ballerina was Françoise Prévost. Just as great dancers do today, she passed on what she had learned to her pupils. Two of them, Marie-Anne Cupis de Camargo and Marie Sallé, became the most famous ballerinas of the time.

La Camargo (as she became known) made a strong and sudden entry on to the ballet scene when at the last minute she danced a solo in place of a male dancer who had failed to appear. She had brilliant technique, with lightning-quick footwork. Sallé's technique was not as brilliant, but her delicate grace and touching acting made her a popular favourite. The two became great rivals.

They both had great influence on the clothes ballerinas wore on stage. La Camargo was proud of her tiny feet; her shoemaker made a fortune by selling 'Camargo Shoes' to ladies who thought they would make their own feet look smaller. She was also proud of the unique steps she had mastered, such as the *entrechat quatre*. But because of the long skirts ballerinas wore, audiences could hardly see her perform these jumps in which she quickly crossed and uncrossed her feet. La Camargo had the perfect answer: she shortened her skirts.

Sallé was just as adventurous. In London, where she was dancing in *Pygmalion*, she appeared in a flimsy Greek tunic and sandals which had been forbidden at the Paris Opéra. Such a thing had never been seen on the ballet stage and it was to be another fifteen years before Parisians could see the sight.

In London in the early eighteenth century dancing master John Weaver produced shows that told stories through dance and mime. These became popular across Europe, staged by people such as the Austrian, Franz Hilferding, who wanted to free dance from the strict rules of the opera ballet. Another man who wanted to do the same was Jean-Georges Noverre.

In 1760 Noverre published his *Lettres* in which he put down the ideas that he hoped would change court dance into a theatre art. He wanted to alter those costumes that made it difficult to dance. He wanted to do away with the masks that meant that choreographers could not create characters and the dancers could not show any emotions. He wrote, 'Let us have more truth and more realism, and dancing will appear to much greater advantage.'

Although he did not use the words, the ballets he wanted to make were to become known as *ballets d'action*

*The Japanese dancer Hideo Fukagawa as Colas
in Frederick Ashton's* La Fille Mal Gardée.

(story ballets). Noverre became ballet master in Stuttgart,
where he produced a series of magnificent ballets, many
based on Greek legends such as the story of Jason and
Medea. He then moved to Vienna before becoming director of ballet at the Paris Opéra.

One of Noverre's students was Jean Dauberval, and it
was he who produced the first ballet to show ordinary
people. *La Fille Mal Gardée* was first staged in Bordeaux in
1789, using popular tunes of the times. It was a big
success.

The same story, but with different music and
choreography, has been performed ever since. In 1960 Sir

Frederick Ashton created his version for the Royal Ballet at Covent Garden in London. It is still danced there today. Though it must be very different from Dauberval's original, it is linked to Dauberval through the ballerina Tamara Karsavina, who helped Ashton with some scenes. She had danced Petipa's version in Russia at the beginning of this century, and Petipa had seen versions of Dauberval's production early in the last century.

Many French dancers left Paris during the French Revolution and settled in London. One of them, Charles Didelot, a pupil of Dauberval, danced in several ballets by Noverre, and in 1796 staged his own ballet *Zéphyr et Flore*. Until this ballet, male and female dancers performed the same steps. Didelot gave them different steps, to suit their characters, and also introduced simple lifts in the *pas de deux*. He also had dancers attached to wires so that they could fly around the stage!

One of the greatest dancers in Noverre's time was the Italian, Gaetano Vestris. His great ability at jumps and turns earned him the title 'God of the Dance'. He passed on the traditions of the eighteenth-century noble style of dancing to his son, Auguste, who through his own skills also inherited the title.

Auguste Vestris was a brilliant dancer who performed more exciting steps than had ever been seen before. He was also an excellent teacher who encouraged his ballerinas to be more feminine and charming on stage. He passed on his style to his two best pupils, Jules Perrot and August Bournonville. These two men became the great choreographers of the next age of the ballet.

■ The Romantic Ballet

At the end of the eighteenth century and into the nineteenth, writers, artists and composers became fascinated by fantasy and folklore, magical spirits and exotic places. This was known as the Romantic Movement and had great influence on the ballet. This is how Romantic ballets got their name: not from romantic stories of true love. *Swan Lake* is a romantic story, but it is not a Romantic ballet!

The first great Romantic ballerina was an Italian dancer called Marie Taglioni. Marie was the daughter of Filippo Taglioni, an Italian dancing master. He trained her to dance in a light and graceful fashion, giving her classes for up to six hours a day. She first performed in Paris in 1827 in the ballet scene of an opera. Four years later she danced in another, *Robert the Devil*.

The new gas lighting at the Paris Opéra made it possible to light the stage as though it were bathed in mysterious moonlight. Into the soft gloom came a group of nuns, led by Taglioni, to dance in the cloisters of a ruined abbey. They looked as though they belonged to another world, drifting phantom-like through the mists. It was the perfect Romantic image.

This inspired one of the singers to suggest to Marie's father that he should stage a ballet in which Marie really was a creature from another world. He did and the ballet was *La Sylphide*, the first complete Romantic ballet. In it James, a young Scottish farmer, on the eve of his wedding, falls in love with a Sylph, a woodland spirit. They share a few brief moments of happiness until James is tricked by a witch into killing his ideal love.

Taglioni was one of the first ballerinas to dance on the very tips of her toes: *en pointe*, as it is called. Pictures from

Marie Taglioni in The God and the Bayadère.

the time show ballerinas appearing like this, but if you see the very soft pointe shoes they wore, some of which are displayed in theatre museums in London, Paris and Copenhagen, you will realize that they must only have been able to stay on their toes for a fleeting moment.

The Romantic ballet saw the rise of ballerinas such as

Fanny Elssler, Carlotta Grisi, Lucille Grahn and Fanny Cerrito (known in England as Madame Cherrytoes), who were worshipped by their audiences.

Fanny Elssler was born in 1810 into a family of Viennese musicians; her father used to copy out music for the composer Haydn. She made her debut on stage when she was only eight and later travelled throughout Europe, dancing with her sister Thérèse as her partner. In 1834 she was hired by the Opéra in Paris, where she danced many of Taglioni's roles. But her great success came when she introduced the Spanish *Cachucha*, a dance which suited her fiery temperament and fast footwork. She and Taglioni became great rivals. She was the first Romantic ballerina to tour America, a difficult journey then, taking many weeks by sailing ship to get there, and after that travelling in often uncomfortable stage-coaches.

Carlotta Grisi was discovered by Jules Perrot in Naples in 1833. Perrot coached her until she was good enough to appear in Paris, where the poet Théophile Gautier fell in love with her. He persuaded the Paris Opéra to engage her. It was Gautier who thought of creating a ballet based on a story by the German poet Heinrich Heine for her. *Giselle*, which is one of the greatest of Romantic ballets, was first seen in 1841 and has been danced by every major ballet company ever since.

As well as discovering Grisi, Jules Perrot introduced Fanny Cerrito, another Italian dancer, to Paris in 1847. She was strong and lively, not at all romantic to look at, but in Perrot's *Ondine* she was everything audiences had come to expect from their ballerinas. From *Ondine* only the *pas de l'ombre*, when Ondine dances with her shadow, can now be seen, the rest of the ballet having been long forgotten. Sir Frederick Ashton choreographed another version of this ballet in 1958 for Margot Fonteyn – incorporating the *pas de l'ombre* – and that ballet is still performed by the Royal Ballet.

Meanwhile, Auguste Bournonville had settled in Copenhagen as a dancer, choreographer, ballet master and teacher. He was a strong dancer and did not want male dancers to be less important than the ballerinas. Bournonville's style is still important in Denmark and is now appreciated all over the world. Bournonville ballets such as *Napoli*, *Far From Denmark* and *Konservatoriet* have been preserved by the Danes in Copenhagen and are regarded as a priceless heritage. Danish dancers are still taught in the Bournonville tradition, which gives them a light, bouncing technique. They are also excellent at mime, which plays an important part in Bournonville's ballets.

Bournonville saw Taglioni's *La Sylphide* when he was in Paris in 1834. When he staged his own version of the ballet, the sixteen-year-old Lucille Grahn danced the Sylph. She went on to become yet another of Taglioni's rivals.

In 1845, Taglioni, Grahn, Grisi and Cerrito went to London to appear in Jules Perrot's *Pas de Quatre*. Their rivalry was such that they argued for hours over who should have top billing. Benjamin Lumley, the theatre manager, stopped the feuding by suggesting that the oldest should appear first. This was the last great performance of the Romantic ballet.

In 1848, various revolutions in French politics and disturbances throughout Europe drove dancers away from Paris, and the city ceased to be the ballet centre of the world. Audiences who had gone to the Paris Opéra to admire the technique of the dancers now consisted mostly of men, and they went because if they were lucky, they could take the ballerinas out for supper after the performances. Producers of ballet despaired at the lack of interest and began to rely on stage tricks to attract audiences. Ballerinas shared the stage with horses, dogs, huge choirs and aquariums full of real fish. They even danced surrounded by sparkling firework displays.

The only good ballet which has lasted from this bad period in France is *Coppélia*, choreographed by Arthur Saint-Léon, the son of a travelling ballet master, to wonderful music by Léo Delibes. But even in this important ballet, the role of Franz was danced by a girl, to keep the men in the audiences interested. Although *Coppélia* is often danced today, Franz is nowadays always danced by men.

▧ *On to Russia*

In 1730, Anna Ivanovna became Empress of Russia. She was a ruthless ruler, but ballet lovers can be grateful to her for, in 1738, she founded a ballet school to teach her servants' children how to dance for the pleasure of her court. The ballet master was Jean-Baptiste Landé, a Frenchman who had been a dancing master in Sweden. He went to Russia in 1734. There is a story that when he came off the boat he was so impressed by some children he saw dancing on the quay that he persuaded the empress to found her school. True or not, it was Landé who became ballet master of Anna Ivanovna's Imperial Ballet School in St Petersburg, then the capital city, today called Leningrad.

From the school grew the great company known as the

Imperial Ballet of St Petersburg and Moscow. In 1759 the Austrian Franz Hilferding became ballet master of the St Petersburg company. He had produced some of the very first *ballets d'action* in Vienna, and when he arrived in Russia he began to introduce Russian themes into court ballets.

At the beginning of the nineteenth century Charles Didelot came to Russia. He found the pupils of the 'Imperial St Petersburg Theatrical Academy', as Anna Ivanovna's school had come to be called, were studying all theatrical arts, so that if necessary they could sing in operas, play in the orchestra, write out music for musicians, act in plays, shift scenery and dance in ballets. Didelot began to put his own ideas into practice. He wanted dancers to be trained to express themselves through music and convey the meaning of the stories to the audience.

When Napoleon invaded Russia in 1811 Didelot had to flee, but he returned after the French defeat and began to stage ballets using dancers he and his pupils had trained, who were able to interpret dramatic roles. But one of his ballets proved too modern for the tsar and he was asked to retire.

During the following years there were several different ballet masters and Marie Taglioni made her first appearance in St Petersburg, returning to Russia several times and helping to create public enthusiasm for ballet and to inspire Russian dancers. The other great Romantic ballerinas also appeared in Russia: Lucille Grahn made her debut there in 1843 and Fanny Elssler in 1848.

In the same month that Elssler danced for the first time in Russia, Jules Perrot arrived to take over as ballet master. It was in this position that he staged many of his greatest ballets. And he had as his assistant Marius

Petipa, who was to become the single most influential figure in the story of classical ballet.

When Perrot left in 1858 he was succeeded by Arthur Saint-Léon, the man who was in 1870 to create *Coppélia* for the Paris Opéra. He referred to himself a 'Jack of all trades', and he certainly was one: he could dance well (indeed, he partnered Taglioni, Cerrito and Grahn), produce ballets, compose music, and he was an excellent violinist. He once played the violin while dancing, in a ballet called *The Violin of the Devil*.

But Russian audiences soon became tired of the ballets Saint-Léon staged for them: they had seen all that sort of thing before. But in 1864 he put on a new ballet – *The Little Humpedbacked Horse*. It was based on a well-known Russian folktale, and was a great success. He also introduced into it exciting dances from many parts of Russia – the sort of folk dances that he would use again in *Coppélia*.

When Saint-Léon returned to Paris in 1869, Marius Petipa was appointed First Ballet Master. He ruled Russian ballet for nearly thirty-five years, until he retired in 1903.

Petipa's father had been a ballet master who in 1848 became a teacher at the St Petersburg School. In Paris his brother Lucien had created the role of Albrecht in *Giselle* in 1841, and he greatly overshadowed Marius as a dancer. But even so in 1847 Marius left Paris and went to St Petersburg as *premier danseur*.

His first important ballet, *The Daughter of Pharaoh*, choreographed in 1861, was a success, and *La Bayadère*, created in 1877, was an even bigger success. The 'Kingdom of the Shades' scene is still danced by many companies today. But again, the audiences soon became bored. So Petipa brought in ballerinas from Italy, where

Carlo Blasis was training dancers who were technically brilliant, especially in their pointe work. Blasis's dancers had developed extremely strong legs and ankles, and it was for these dancers that the first proper pointe shoes as we might know them today were produced – ballet slippers which had stiffened soles and toe-pieces. It was one of these Italian stars, Virginia Zucchi, who revived interest in ballet among Russian audiences when she danced in St Petersburg in 1885. She completely dazzled the audiences (and she also stimulated a deep love of ballet in Alexander Benois, a Russian artist, writer and ballet designer, who in turn passed his love of ballet on to the young Serge Diaghilev, with important results in the future as we shall see). When she danced for a season in Moscow, takings at the box office doubled.

Another important person who was to have a lasting influence on ballet also came to Russia at this time: Enrico Cecchetti, a brilliant Italian dancer who became Second Ballet Master to the Imperial Theatres. He was a great teacher with Diaghilev's company after the Russian Revolution. But Diaghilev's story comes later.

We are now in the great age of the classical ballet, a description which is sometimes confusing as it can be used in two different ways. Just as you can describe ballets as Romantic, referring to the period and style in which they were made, and also romantic, referring to the story, classical can refer to the whole style of ballet technique, in particular the use of point work, and it can also refer to the glorious period of ballet history towards the end of the nineteenth century, when Petipa was creating the grand ballets such as *The Sleeping Beauty* in Moscow and Leningrad.

By 1880, the Director of the Imperial Theatres was on the point of dismissing Petipa for, despite loving Zucchi, audiences were not coming to the theatres to see what Petipa was offering them. He decided to give Petipa one more chance and chose the story of *The Sleeping Beauty*, a fairy tale by the seventeenth-century Frenchman, Charles Perrault, to display both Petipa's talents as a choreographer and the strength and talents of Russian dancers.

He persuaded Tchaikovsky, then at the height of his fame, to write the music. Tchaikovsky was reluctant to do so, because his first ballet, *Swan Lake*, which had been produced in 1877 for the Bolshoi Theatre in Moscow, by a choreographer named Reisinger, had been a failure. But eventually he agreed, and asked Petipa to write down exactly what he wanted. Petipa did just that, making notes that told the composer exactly what was to happen on stage at every moment.

The first Aurora, the Sleeping Beauty, was another Italian dancer, Carlotta Brianzi. Cecchetti created the roles of the Bluebird and the wicked fairy Carabosse. The ballet was a great success, but Tsar Alexander only said, 'Very nice.'

It was decided that Petipa and Tchaikovsky should work together again on *The Nutcracker*, to be based on a story by E. T. A. Hoffmann. Tchaikovsky disliked the music he wrote for it. Petipa became ill before he could choreograph the ballet, so the work was done by his assistant, Lev Ivanov. Ivanov was that rare thing in the story of Russian ballet at this time: he was actually Russian. It's odd that *The Nutcracker*, which is probably the most famous ballet in the world, was, like *Swan Lake*, not a great success when it was first produced in 1892!

Tchaikovsky died of cholera in 1893. For a memorial concert for the composer in 1894, Ivanov staged Act II of

The Snowflakes in the original production of The Nutcracker
at the Maryinsky Theatre in St Petersburg (Leningrad) in 1892.

Swan Lake, 'The Flight of the Swans'. It was the success of
the evening and Tsar Nicholas II ordered that the whole
ballet be revived.

The two lakeside acts of the ballet in which the swans
appear are called the white acts. Ivanov choreographed
both of them while Petipa choreographed the grand court
scenes of Acts I and III.

The first performance of this re-choreographed ballet
was in January 1895. The Swan Queen was the Italian
dancer Pierina Legnani who had astonished St Petersburg audiences two years earlier when, in *Cinderella*, she
had performed thirty-two consecutive *fouettés*. She repeated the feat in Act III of *Swan Lake* when, in the second
part of her double role, as Odile (the Black Swan), she
fools the prince into believing that she is his beloved
Odette (the White Swan), whom he has sworn to love.

Sadly, Ivanov died penniless and forgotten in 1901.
Petipa, who choreographed more than sixty ballets, after

his retirement in 1903 lived on until 1910. He had completely dominated Russian ballet for almost fifty years. In that time he created over fifty ballets, as well as reviving almost twenty old ones and making the dances for about thirty-five operas. He had also created the 'Russian' style of dance based on brilliant technique, which we still see today. It is also the style that has been developed in different directions by the great choreographers of this century: Frederick Ashton and George Balanchine.

At the end of the nineteenth century, while Petipa was still producing brilliant ballets, audiences were becoming bored once again and young people in the ballet world were trying to break free from the strict classicism of the Imperial Theatre.

■ Ballet in the Twentieth Century

When Mikhail Fokine graduated from the Imperial Ballet School and joined the St Petersburg company in 1898 he was very unhappy with the roles he was asked to dance. He thought that the choreography was boring and the ballets artificial.

In 1904 he sent a suggestion for a ballet on the story of *Daphnis and Chloe* to the Director of the Imperial Theatres. He said that as the ballet was on a historical subject everything should be as it would have been during that period in history. He didn't want his ballerinas to wear tutus and pointe shoes as they always did in the Imperial Theatre, whether they were meant to be Indian princesses or gypsy queens. His idea was turned down.

In 1907 he choreographed a ballet called *Eunice*. He insisted that the dancers appear barefoot on stage. But bare legs and feet were forbidden, so the dancers had to wear flesh-coloured tights and on the tights they painted toes!

Later that year, Fokine worked with Alexander Benois, and through him met Serge Diaghilev. Diaghilev, the son of rich parents, had been sent to St Petersburg to study law. There he met Benois and the painter Léon Bakst. The three, together with their other intellectual friends, were always talking about the arts. Diaghilev put on art exhibitions in St Petersburg and later on in Paris where, in 1906, he organized a successful exhibition of Russian art. The next year he arranged a series of concerts of Russian music which were so successful that the famous Russian singer Feodor Chaliapin was asked to bring a complete opera to Paris. Diaghilev supervised the staging of the opera, *Boris Gudunov*, in 1908, and it was a triumph.

The following year, again in Paris, Diaghilev put on a programme of ballets and one act from the opera *Prince Igor* at the Theatre du Châtelet. Fokine choreographed the Polovtsian Dances in the opera, filling the stage with hordes of leaping Tartar warriors. The whole event, especially Fokine's dances, was a sensation. And it was this performance that marks the rebirth of ballet outside Russia. Parisians flocked to see the dancers Diaghilev had brought with him, including Anna Pavlova, Tamara Karsavina and Vaslav Nijinsky.

The season he staged the following year, 1910, was an even greater triumph. Audiences were amazed by Fokine's *Firebird* with music by Stravinsky and by his *Scheherazade* with Léon Bakst's astonishing designs.

The only failure of the season was *Giselle*, which Paris audiences found rather old-fashioned when compared to the other offerings on the programme. When he returned to Russia, Nijinsky wore the same costume in *Giselle* that he had worn in Paris. The dowager empress was shocked

*Vaslav Nijinsky as the Golden Slave
in Mikhail Fokine's* Scheherazade.

by the way it revealed the dancer's body and the company imposed a fine on him. Nijinsky refused to pay it and was fired.

Diaghilev then founded a permanent Ballets Russes company to show off Nijinsky's genius. He engaged other dancers from the Imperial Theatres in St Petersburg and Moscow and set off on a triumphant tour of European capitals.

Diaghilev encouraged Nijinsky to start choreographing. In 1912 Nijinsky's first ballet, L'Après-Midi d'un Faun (The Afternoon of a Faun) was staged in Paris. Fokine became jealous of Nijinsky and left the company. Although a brilliant classical dancer, Nijinsky did not create in the classical style. Instead, he worked out his own movements, which are more like modern dance than ballet. They caused great scandals, particularly Le Sacre du Printemps (The Rite of Spring) which caused a riot in the theatre. It was not just Nijinsky's choreography that caused the outcry. Igor Stravinsky's very modern, 'un-melodic' music offended the audiences of the time.

And then Nijinsky sailed to South America to tour with the company. On board ship he met Romola de Pulszky and married her. From that moment on Diaghilev refused to have anything to do with Nijinsky, although when he was interned in Hungary in World War I, as an enemy alien, Diaghilev worked to have him released. Nijinsky joined the company for its American tour in the winter of 1916, but he was already showing signs of the mental illness which led to total insanity in 1919. He never danced again.

After Nijinsky's departure, Diaghilev persuaded Fokine to rejoin the company to choreograph the ballet The Legend of Joseph and hired a young dancer from Moscow, Léonide Massine, to dance the role of Joseph.

Massine was to become one of the most successful choreographers of his time, with ballets such as *La Boutique Fantasque* and *The Good-Humoured Ladies*.

When war broke out in 1914, most of the Ballets Russes dancers returned to Russia. But somehow Diaghilev kept the company going and after the war the company appeared in London and again toured all over Europe.

Into the 1920s Diaghilev continued to discover new talent, including Anton Dolin and the fourteen-year-old Alicia Markova from England. From Russia came a young soloist called Georgi Balanchivadze (who would change his name to Balanchine) and a glamorous young dancer, Serge Lifar.

After ten years of astounding the public with exotic Russian ballets, Diaghilev had difficulty thinking up some new sensation every season. In the 1920s he had ballets with plastic sets, ballets with music written for the clattering of typewriters and smart ballets set on the beach. By 1929 the strain became too great and, while in Venice to rest after the exertions of the season, he died. He was buried on the cemetery island of San Michele. Over forty years later his friend and collaborator Stravinsky was buried near him.

■ Ballet Around the World

Diaghilev's death while his company was on holiday meant that the dancers were scattered all over Europe. But even before his death another great ballerina, Anna Pavlova, had been taking ballet around the world.

The daughter of a laundress, she graduated from the Imperial Ballet School in St Petersburg and soon became a ballerina. Fokine created *The Dying Swan* for her in 1907 and she danced in some of Diaghilev's early seasons in Paris.

But she preferred to have her own company and tour the world. She settled in London and bought Ivy House in Hampstead in 1912. (It is now the Pavlova Museum.) Her passion was to take ballet to places and people that had never seen ballet before. She liked Britain and, for her corps de ballet, British girls, who remained quiet and polite as they put up with the tremendous hardships of touring across America, to Japan, Australia and New Zealand. They even agreed to change their names to ones that sounded more Russian – Hilda Munnings became, rather unfortunately, Munningsova before a complete change made her Lydia Sokolova.

In Hollywood Pavlova made a silent film with Douglas Fairbanks as well as filming some of her short solos such as *The Poppy*, in which she wrapped herself up in great red petals, or as a Firefly – to keep her Dying Swan company.

She died in The Hague, in Holland, in 1931, typically enough, while on tour, leaving behind her an enormous audience whom she had introduced to the ballet, and a lot of dancers she had trained who were to go on to found ballet schools all over the world.

■ The Ballets Russes

There were several attempts to keep the Ballets Russes name alive in the 1930s, mostly companies organized by the colourful characters Colonel de Basil, who arranged the business side, and René Blum, who looked after the artistic side. They spent a great deal of time arguing and taking each other to court to decide who owned which ballets and who could dance what. They performed Léonide Massine's new sort of ballet, the symphonic ballet, danced to symphonies by composers such as Tchaikovsky, Brahms and Berlioz.

In 1933 they also introduced the three 'baby ballerinas', Baronova (thirteen years old), Toumanova (fourteen) and Riabouchinska (fifteen), to the public. In the late 1930s and early 1940s the Ballets Russes spent much time in America. Mikhail Fokine created his last ballet for them before he died in 1942, and for a time their ballerina was Alicia Markova.

■ British Ballet

After Diaghilev's death Alicia Markova returned home to Britain without any idea of what she would do. As things turned out, she went back at exactly the right time to be in at the start of British ballet.

Marie Rambert, a Polish dancer who had helped Nijinsky put on *Le Sacre du Printemps* in Paris, married an Englishman and started a school in London in 1920. Ninette de Valois, from Ireland, who had also danced for Diaghilev, founded a school when she returned to Britain in 1926. That same year she started putting on the dances for the Old Vic Theatre and then, in 1931, for the Sadler's Wells Theatre. And so the Vic-Wells Ballet was formed.

This became the Sadler's Wells Theatre Ballet, with Markova as the prima ballerina, partnered by Anton Dolin. Margot Fonteyn entered the school at the age of fourteen in 1933 and became their ballerina in 1934 when Markova left. Robert Helpmann, who had come from Australia to join the company, became Fonteyn's first regular partner.

Ninette de Valois.

When the theatre was bombed in the Second World War, the company changed its name to the Sadler's Wells Ballet and, in 1956, after it moved into the Royal Opera House, Covent Garden, and was given a Royal Charter, it became the Royal Ballet.

Marie Rambert started a company in 1930 and discovered many young choreographers, including Frederick Ashton and Antony Tudor. Her small company continues dancing today, although in 1966 it became a modern dance company, now called the Rambert Dance Company.

After touring and dancing for long periods in America, Alicia Markova and Anton Dolin started Festival Ballet at the time of the Festival of Britain in 1951, and they brought many foreign dancers to Britain for the first time.

Elizabeth West and Peter Darrell started Western Theatre Ballet in 1957 to produce ballets on new, more dramatic, subjects. When this little company had to break up in 1966, some dancers went on to form Northern Ballet in Manchester and Peter Darrell founded the Scottish Ballet with his ballerina, Elaine McDonald. She became Artistic Co-ordinator after his death in 1987.

In 1978 Harold King started London City Ballet after giving lunchtime performances. This company now dances in small theatres all over Britain and has the Princess of Wales as a very active Patron.

Britain's influence in ballet is also felt in Australia and Canada, where there are several important companies. The two national companies were started with the advice of Ninette de Valois, founder of the great Royal Ballet.

■ Australia and New Zealand

There is a history of dance in Australia that goes back to pre-history. Aboriginal ritual dances are some of the oldest known to man. But ballet or theatrical dance did not come to the continent until the 1840s when, not so long after it was created (considering the distance), performances of *La Sylphide* were given.

The Australian Ballet of today is the result of dancers from Pavlova's company settling there when she toured the country in the late twenties. The most important was Borovansky, who opened a school in Melbourne, and, later, a small company which lasted until his death in 1959.

The last season was directed by Peggy van Praagh,

who had worked with the Sadler's Wells Ballet. Together with good young soloists from Borovansky, including Marilyn Jones and Garth Welch, she became founding Artistic Director of the Australian Ballet, which gave its first performances in 1962. In 1964 the company founded a school which produces many fine dancers. Sir Robert Helpmann, the first true Australian to direct the company, joined in 1965 after the enormous success of one of his ballets, *The Display*.

The Australian Ballet is now directed by Maina Gielgud, once a great dramatic ballerina with companies such as Maurice Béjart's Ballet of the Twentieth Century and London Festival Ballet. The Australians have a very high standard and a good repertoire in spite of being so far away from most other ballet centres. In 1988 they gave a brilliantly successful season at the Royal Opera House, London, to celebrate Australia's 200th birthday.

They were joined in the season by the modern dance company, Sydney Dance Theatre. Its director, Graeme Murphy, has created dances for both companies, a successful example of cooperation between two schools of dance.

New Zealand is almost too small a country to have a ballet company of its own, but all the same, one has existed since 1953. There are several dancers from New Zealand in international companies, including Martin James of London Festival Ballet.

■ *Canada*

Dance in Canada started in 1938 with the founding of the Winnipeg Ballet, which has the distinction of being the first ballet company to receive a royal charter, after performing before the queen in 1953. They have a wide repertoire, including many ballets with Canadian subjects, such as one which involves Canadian square-dancing.

The bigger National Ballet of Canada was formed in 1951 by the Englishwoman Celia Franca, who was hired by the governors on the advice of Dame Ninette de Valois. It is now a major international company with a very impressive school which has produced many good dancers, including Karen Kain and Frank Augustyn, who still lead the company. They have produced many good three-act ballets, including *Napoli* by Peter Schaufuss, and have been directed by such famous ballet personalities as Alexander Grant who previously had been a brilliant character dancer with the Royal Ballet, and the great Danish classical dancer, Erik Bruhn.

■ *Europe*

In France Serge Lifar ran the Paris Opéra from 1930, after leaving the Diaghilev company, until 1945. He improved the school, which went on to produce many great ballerinas, including Yvette Chauviré. The ballet company at the Opéra is now directed by Rudolf Nureyev.

One student of the Opéra school was Roland Petit, who worked with the Ballets de Champs Elysées before forming his own company, the Ballets de Paris in 1948. His glamorous wife, Zizi Jeanmaire, is the star of many of his ballets, the best-known of which is *Carmen*. He also choreographed and both danced in many revues and films such as *Hans Christian Andersen*. Petit is now director of the Ballet de Marseille, producing witty and theatrical ballets, including his own version of *Coppélia*.

In Denmark the Royal Danish Ballet carefully looked after Bournonville's ballets, which still form the biggest part of the company's repertoire.

Sweden has a ballet tradition that dates back to the seventeenth century, and the Royal Swedish Ballet still perform some of the old works in a little royal theatre at Drottningholm which was discovered lying untouched two hundred years after it was built. The original stage machinery was still in place and all that had to be replaced were the ropes that made the marvellous quick changes work.

The Royal Swedish Ballet of today has many excellent young dancers, but they do not often tour, preferring to stay at home performing in a very good repertoire of works from choreographers worldwide. There is a more adventurous company in Gothenburg directed until 1988 by Ulf Gadd.

Germany played an important part in the development of modern dance in the 1930s and it was not until after the Second World War that classical ballet grew in importance. Now there are many small companies attached to the dozens of opera houses across the country. The biggest are in Berlin, Stuttgart (which was more important when John Cranko, who died in 1973, was the director) and in Hamburg, where John Neumeier has a marvellous company, that mostly dances his choreography.

And what of Italy, where all this ballet activity started over four hundred years ago? Unfortunately, there are now no companies of world importance. But Aterballetto, a small company based in Regio Emilio, has made a lot of progress recently, and the country has produced ballerinas of international reputation, such as Carla Fracci and Elisabetta Terabust, who dance as guest artists with many companies.

■ *Russia*

A lot of Russia's dance talent left in the first two decades of this century, first with Diaghilev and then after the Revolution of 1917. Few returned home. But those who stayed managed to convince the Commissar of the Arts that ballet should not be done away with, and new choreographers emerged who made ballets about the problems of the working classes to please the new régime. But slowly the classic ballets began to appear again. The choreographer Leonid Lavrovsky created *Romeo and Juliet* for Galina Ulanova, a great Soviet ballerina, and, indeed, one of the greatest dancers of this century. This ballet is typical of the new big, Bolshoi style (*bolshoi* is Russian for big) that found a home in Moscow. One of their most popular ballets is Yuri Grigorovich's version of *Spartacus*, the story of a slaves' revolt in ancient Rome, and it is danced to Khatchaturian's exciting music. Moscow became the centre of Soviet ballet, while the Leningrad company (now renamed the Kirov, after a Soviet politician) kept alive the pure classical style of the Imperial Ballet of tsarist days.

Russia has over thirty-five companies in smaller cities and towns, and, many of these companies produce great dancers, such as Nadezhda Pavlova who trained in Perm, and who now performs with the Bolshoi.

■ Down the Generations

The Danish tradition founded by Bournonville is the best example of the way ballets are handed down from generation to generation and the changes which happen to them on the way. Sometimes the process is like the party game of Chinese Whispers, with parts of ballets changing as dancers each remember the same ballets slightly differently. There were no films or videos to keep a record in Bournonville's day and the different types of notation (ways of writing down ballets) in use at that time could be interpreted in different ways.

When Bournonville was directing the Royal Danish Ballet he was also, for the first twenty years, the leading male dancer – a very strong male dancer. He made roles for himself which had a lot of dancing. But when he stopped dancing he changed the steps in his ballets to give the male dancers of that time less to do. This may have been because they were not as talented as he was, or perhaps he did not want them to overshadow him!

As Denmark was a small country, away from the main centres of dance, the Royal Danish Ballet looked after their own ballets and many were handed down from dancer to dancer so that some, such as *La Sylphide*, have never been out of the repertoire in almost 150 years. After Bournonville's death in 1879, his ballets were looked after by ballet masters and dancers. At the end of the nineteenth century Hans Beck rescued some which were in danger of being lost. In the early decades of this century his pupil, Harald Lander, took over the task. After him there have been many others who have not only looked after Bournonville's ballets, but have also taken them to many other countries. So from Bournonville to today has taken a chain of only four generations.

Some Bournonville ballets have lasted only as fragments, or with acts missing. For example in *Napoli* the second act became neglected as the audience thought it so boring that they went to the famous restaurant Bronnums next to theatre while it was being performed. It became known as the Bronnums Act! If you see this act today it will be a modern version created in the style of the original version.

As male dancing has improved, many choreographers have made the male characters in Bournonville's ballets as important as they originally were. Perhaps the steps are now even more virtuoso, but they are always in the Bournonville style. This is good for dancing as ballet should not be kept as a museum piece. It has to change with the times.

■ USA

In 1930 George Balanchine was offered the position of Director of the Paris Opéra Ballet, but he decided to go to Britain instead. There he formed a small company, the Ballet 1933, but it did not last long, and when he was invited to America by Lincoln Kirstein, an interested amateur, to found a company, he accepted eagerly. But first, he said, he must found a school.

Within six months his students had given their first performance, and they were soon formed into a company and became connected to the Metropolitan Opera in New York. In 1941 dancers from this group joined another company, the American Ballet Caravan, to tour South America, dancing ballets which included the all-American *Billy the Kid*, choreographed by Eugene Loring with music by Aaron Copland.

In 1946 the Ballet Society was formed from this group started by Balanchine to show new ballets choreographed by Balanchine and others. Later they were able to give performances at the New York City Center. Their first appearance as the New York City Ballet was in 1948.

The company danced many works by Balanchine, and in 1949 Jerome Robbins joined as both dancer and choreographer. He had made his early ballets, such as *Fancy Free*, for American Ballet Theater, which had been founded by Lucia Chase in 1939. Ballet Theater performed ballets by Fokine, Anton Dolin, Agnes de Mille and Antony Tudor, who had moved to New York from Britain. Alicia Markova became one of its stars and a little later the company produced its own ballerina, the Cuban, Alicia Alonso, who now directs the Cuban Ballet.

Ballet Theater toured America over the years, creating a big, new audience. Soon many other companies were being formed in cities such as Boston, Pittsburgh and San Francisco. Now almost every city of any size has a company, no matter how small, even if it can only afford to perform *The Nutcracker* every Christmas.

Today classical ballet is danced in most countries of the world. Even China has a classical ballet company and Japan has dozens of them. Only a hundred years ago ballet was performed for a privileged few. Now it is there for everyone to enjoy.

■ MODERN DANCE

Towards the end of the nineteenth century, when classical ballet was at a peak, some people began to think that dance had become too formal. They wanted to free it from old-fashioned ideas and make it more natural. Many of the people who were putting forward these new ideas came from the New World – America.

Loie Fuller was born in the state of Illinois in 1862. She was an actress, singer, playwright, theatre producer and self-taught dancer. But she did not dance like the classical ballerinas of the time. She moved in a very free way dressed in yards and yards of coloured silk, on stages lit by multi-coloured lights. She was like a moving sculpture.

When she danced in Paris for the first time, in 1892, she was an enormous success. At the beginning of the new century she began to create works for groups of dancers, and in 1908, twenty years before she died, she founded a school to teach her ideas to others.

One of the women who saw Loie Fuller perform was Isadora Duncan, who is now a legend in the world of modern dance. Born in San Francisco in 1877, she was inspired by the way trees moved in the wind and the waves of the sea. She was also influenced by the writings of François Delsarte, a French acting teacher. In 1899 she arrived in London with her family. There she saw the Greek sculptures in the British Museum for the first time, which inspired her even more.

While she was in London, Isadora met Mrs Patrick Campbell, a famous actress and great friend of the playwright George Bernard Shaw. 'Mrs Pat' introduced the American girl to many of her friends and eventually Isadora gave a recital of her dancing for them. Soon no smart party in London was complete unless Isadora Duncan was there to entertain the guests.

From London she moved to Paris, where she was a sensation. Loie Fuller organized Isadora's first tour of Europe: wherever she danced she was the talk of the town. She travelled as far as St Petersburg, where Diaghilev and Fokine saw her dance. They were impressed and so, without realizing it at the time, she had an influence on the way classical ballet would change. The young ballerina Tamara Karsavina wrote about her visit in her biography *Theatre Street*.

Isadora opened a school near Berlin and planned enormous performances in which hundreds of children would dance to music such as Beethoven's Choral Symphony.

She met the American millionaire Paris Singer (who had made his money from Singer Sewing Machines), and he bought her beautiful premises for her school in Paris in 1908. With the outbreak of the First World War, in 1914, the Paris school was evacuated to New York, but later returned to Europe – at first to Switzerland and then back to Paris. In 1921 the new Communist government of Russia asked her to start a school in Moscow. She agreed and in Moscow she danced with her pupils at the Bolshoi Theatre. When Lenin died in 1924, she choreographed two dances for his funeral. Then she set off for the Ukraine, handing out what money she earned to the poor. Later that year, now poverty-stricken herself (not for the first time) she left Russia and returned to France, where she died in 1927.

Isadora Duncan was as famous for her scandalous behaviour as she was for her dancing, but she did encourage other dancers to break away from the rigid ideas of ballet and explore freer relationships between music and movement.

Among the people she influenced was Rudolf von Laban who was an assistant of the Swiss composer Emile Dalcroze, who had been a pupil of Délibes (the composer of the music for *Coppélia*). Dalcroze invented a system

Lynn Seymour in Brahms Waltzes *created by Frederick Ashton in the style of Isadora Duncan.*

called eurythmics to help his students develop a sense of rhythm based on the relationship between sounds and physical movement.

He invented his system mainly for musicians, but he and Laban, who was much more theatrical, came to realize that the system could be useful for dancers. Dalcroze and Laban were among the first to teach modern dance as a theory at Dalcroze's school at Dresden in Germany.

One of the women who studied with Dalcroze and Laban was Mary Wigman, who later became Laban's assistant before opening her own school in Dresden. Mary Wigman did not look at all like a dancer: she was strong and muscular. And she did not believe in movement for movement's sake: everything she did on stage or choreographed for others had to mean something. One of her pupils, Hanya Holm, settled in New York, where she opened the Mary Wigman Studio in 1931. Later she would choreograph the musical *My Fair Lady*.

Another person who was inspired by Isadora Duncan was Maud Allan. She was born in Canada and came to Europe to study music in Berlin. She became fascinated by modern dance and, although she had no formal training, she became one of the most daring dancers of her generation. When she appeared in *Vision of Salomé* her transparent skirt caused a scandal. And at the end of the ballet, when she was holding John the Baptist's severed head on a salver, she pressed her lips against it. This gesture was much too dramatic for her first-night audience and she was forced to make changes.

The fourth American woman who made an important contribution at the birth of modern dance was Ruth St Denis. When she was a child her mother, who had studied with a Delsarte teacher like Loie Fuller, gave Ruth her first dancing lessons. She later went to dance school and became a professional dancer, often appearing in musicals.

When she was on tour in Europe with a show called *Dubarry* she saw a poster advertising cigarettes, with a picture of an Egyptian goddess on it. This gave her the idea of exploring Oriental dances and themes, and adapting them to modern dance. Her first work, *Rahda*, was a Hindu story. But rather than use Hindu music, which might have bored her audience, she cleverly used music by Délibes. She had a big success and could have stayed in Europe and worked there constantly, but she preferred to return to the United States to appear in vaudeville theatres. In 1915 she and her husband, Ted Shawn, opened the Denishawn School of Dancing and Related Arts in Los Angeles.

Ted Shawn had taken dance classes to strengthen his legs after he had been ill. He became so interested in dance that he gave up studying to go into the church and became a full-time dancer. He first saw Ruth St Denis dance in 1911 and they were married in 1914.

It was from the Denishawn School that most of the modern dance you see today comes. All forms of dance, including Oriental and ballet (but not pointe work), were taught at the school. The Denishawn Company also gave many successful performances.

In 1932 Ruth St Denis and Ted Shawn separated, and in 1940 the school closed down. But by this time thousands of people had been taught modern dance. These Denishawn dancers did not offer audiences shows of light and silk as Loie Fuller had done, nor the ethnic dances from the Orient that had inspired Ruth St Denis. They offered straightforward modern dance; its style was as plain and severe as the clothes they usually performed in.

Ruth St Denis performed until she was in her eighties and died at the grand old age of ninety.

Possibly the most important graduate of the Denishawn School was Martha Graham. She was nearly twenty years old before her family allowed her to go to the Denishawn School for a summer course. Later, when she was an established member of the Denishawn Company, she realized that to fulfil her potential as a dancer she had to have something to dance about. Denishawn taught dance as a means of putting a message across to the audience. Graham agreed with this, of course, but she was not sure what their message was.

In 1923 she left Denishawn and went to New York, where she danced in revues and taught for some time before giving her first performance in April 1926. She immediately established herself as an important modern dancer-choreographer and became the leading force in the creation of American modern dance. She opened a studio where she worked out what is now known as Graham Technique. Martha Graham's ballets often show powerful women from the Bible and from Greek mythology, such as Jocasta, Medea, Judith and Clytemnestra.

But one of her lasting masterpieces was created before she found inspiration in these characters. It is *Appalachian Spring*, choreographed in 1944 – the simple story of a young settler and his wife taking possession of their new home in America. With music by Aaron Copland and a plain set, it typified all that Martha Graham stood for. It is still danced today, and in a recent performance the classical dancers Rudolf Nureyev and Mikhail Baryshnikov played the roles of the fiery preacher and the young husband.

Martha Graham was a magnetic performer who did not stop dancing until 1973, when she was almost eighty. Even then she did not retire, but devoted her extraordinary energies to running her company and her school. Among her pupils and dancers are many who have gone on to found their own modern companies.

Merce Cunningham and Paul Taylor are just two of these. Cunningham created one of the leading roles in *Appalachian Spring* a year before he left the company. By then he had given several solo performances in New

*Martha Graham as Jocasta and Bertram Ross
as Oedipus in Graham's* Night Journey.

York and continued with his solo career after he left the Graham company. In 1953 the Merce Cunningham Dance Company gave its first performance. Six years later, he opened his own studio in New York. Today, his company is one of the leading modern-dance groups in the world. Cunningham was deeply influenced by the Martha Graham style and technique, but he does not make dances with stories or about heroic people. Dance, he says, can be its own subject matter. He works a lot with the American composer John Cage who writes unusual pieces in which the players hit their instruments or simply don't play for long periods.

Paul Taylor had danced with the Merce Cunningham Company and had formed his own company before he joined Martha Graham in 1955. He is now one of the most important modern-dance choreographers. His ballets appear to be much more classical than those of many of today's modern-dance choreographers. Although he does not use formal ballet technique in his works, several of them are in the repertoires of major 'classical' companies. And many of them are the most enjoyable in the world of modern dance, as he is one of the few modern choreographers with a sense of humour. Many are very serious indeed.

Another of today's leading modern-dance figures is Twyla Tharp, who studied with Merce Cunningham. Her early works, performed without music, were often danced in unusual locations, such as gyms and art galleries. In 1971 she used the music of jazz pianist Jelly Roll Morton for her ballet *Eight Jelly Rolls*, which established her as an important modern-dance figure. She now mixes jazz, pop and social dance with virtuoso ballet technique. This was shown at its best in *Push Comes to Shove*, in which Mikhail Baryshnikov did crazy things with a bowler hat.

In Britain, modern dance had a late start. It was not until 1969 that Robert Cohan, Martha Graham's one-time partner, was invited to London to found a modern-dance company. The result was London Contemporary Dance Theatre, which performs widely and has an important school.

But three years before LCDT was founded, Britain's oldest dance company, Ballet Rambert, changed from being a classical company to a modern-dance one, under the direction of Norman Morrice. The company had been founded many years before by Marie Rambert who, as a student in Paris in the early years of the century, had arranged dances for herself in the style of Isadora

Duncan. The company introduced many American modern choreographers to Britain and discovered some of its own. In 1987 it changed its name to the Rambert Dance Company and it is now directed by Richard Alston, who received his training at Eton and the London Contemporary Dance Theatre.

One of the best known of Rambert's dancers and choreographers was Christopher Bruce: he is now resident choreographer with London Festival Ballet. This company is typical of many of the leading 'classical' ballet companies which dance the works of modern-dance choreographers such as Paul Taylor and Glen Tetley alongside their classical ballets.

Tamara Karsavina's thought at the beginning of this century that modern dance and classical should share a stage has, at last, come true.

▌ PUTTING ON YOUR WHITE TIE . . . ▌ DANCE ON STAGE AND SCREEN

Many people first see dancing as part of a stage show or in a film. There is a good chance that the first time you saw it was at a pantomime or the ballet as a Christmas treat. Or perhaps on television in a popular show.

Stage shows with dancing are almost as old as the ballet, but not, of course, in the form we see them today. Dancing was used as a *divertissement* – an entertainment – in the show and it was not until well into this century that the big, popular musical show with a story developed.

Variety shows (called music-hall in Britain, vaudeville in America) often had ballet items in the programme. The great Danish ballerina Adeline Genée, who would become one of the founders of the Royal Academy of

Dancing, was the leading dancer at the Empire Theatre in London for ten years, and even Pavlova and Nijinsky appeared on variety bills at big theatres such as the London Coliseum – alongside jugglers, animal acts and singers.

One of the earliest musical shows with popular dances was *The Black Crook*, which was produced in New York in 1866. It was a fantastic story of an alchemist who made a pact with the Devil to deliver him one soul for every year of his life. It was a series of numbers with elaborate scenery and was really more like a revue than a musical.

The dances in musicals were more closely related to social dancing, the dances people do for pleasure, than to ballet, although as the years have gone by the technique of stage dancers has improved enormously. Nowadays they have to be properly trained to be able to perform the steps choreographers create for them.

Even into the 1930s shows were produced with the dance routines inserted into the story to give it some variety. Important choreographers such as George Balanchine created dances, such as in *On Your Toes*, but it was not until the early 1940s that dance was used to tell the story or to explain something about the characters. The first proper ballet in a musical was in the Rodgers and Hammerstein show *Oklahoma!* Agnes de Mille created *Laurie Makes Up Her Mind*, which was a complete ballet showing how Laurie, the heroine, was torn between Curly, her lover, and Jake, who was violently jealous.

Jerome Robbins has been one of the most important people in bringing serious dance into the musical. His 1944 ballet *Fancy Free*, the story of three sailors on shore leave, eventually became the musical *On The Town* (on stage and screen). He also made the *Little House of Uncle*

*A scene from the dance sequence 'Laurie Makes Up Her Mind'
in* Oklahoma! *by Agnes de Mille.*

Tom ballet in the film *The King and I*, in which the King of
Siam is told, through dance, that he is a wicked ruler. In
1957 Robbins created the most perfect dance musical,
West Side Story, in which the dance was as important as
the story and the songs.

Since that time dance has become more and more
important in musicals, the most famous being Andrew
Lloyd Webber's *Cats*, which has starred several leading
dancers from the Royal Ballet, and *Starlight Express*, in
which the dancers sweep about the stage and the theatre
on roller-skates.

The lives of show dancers became the subject of a
musical in *A Chorus Line*, which described the difficult life
dancers have – the auditions, the rehearsals and then the

performances – through brilliant dance routines of every type.

The musical film came with the coming of the talkies. In fact, the very first talkie *was* a musical – Al Jolson sang in *The Jazz Singer* in 1927. This was not a dance film, but within a year or two other musicals were made and dancing was introduced on a large scale. But these films were still often nothing more than stage stars such as Fanny Brice (whose life story was filmed as *Funny Girl*, with Barbra Streisand) doing the acts they performed in vaudeville.

There were big dance routines in *The Hollywood Revue of 1928*, but again they were separate items not connected to a story. By 1930 films were starting to look more like films of today. Stage shows such as *No, No, Nanette* (with its famous song, *Tea for Two*) were filmed, and in 1933 the most famous backstage story of all, *42nd Street*, was made. A dancer called Ginger Rogers played a small comedy role.

For some years before this Fred Astaire had been dancing in famous stage musicals with his sister Adele. Although he was a big stage star, in his first film, *Dancing Lady*, with Joan Crawford, he danced for only a few minutes. In his second film, *Flying Down to Rio*, he danced for only ten minutes, this time with Ginger Rogers. A very important ten minutes these turned out to be, as Rogers and Astaire became the greatest dance partnership the film world had ever seen. They went on to make films such as *The Gay Divorce* (in which he had appeared on stage with Adele) and *Top Hat*, in which they used their versions of ballroom dances to express their characters.

Musical films with elaborate dancing scenes were one

Ginger Rogers and Fred Astaire in Swingtime.

of the most important forms of entertainment in the 1930s and well into the 1940s, with the invention of technicolor. Other favourite dancing stars were the beautiful Jesse Matthews and the elegant Jack Buchanan in Britain and the athletic Gene Kelly in America.

The great choreographers included Astaire, who created most of his own dances, and also worked with Hermes Pan. Busby Berkeley created spectacular kaleidoscopic effects for hundreds of dancers (as well as giant candlesticks and grand pianos!) in films such as *42nd Street*, *Gold Diggers of 1933* and *Dames*.

A few films of ballets have been made, but they have mostly been filmed versions of stage performances. The great exception was *The Red Shoes*, which was made specially for the screen. Based on Hans Christian Andersen's fairy story, it has now become a classic. It showed life in a ballet company for the first time, as well as the cleverly filmed version of the ballet of the red shoes. It starred the beautiful Moira Shearer, who was a ballerina with the Royal Ballet, as well as other famous dancers such as Léonide Massine and Robert Helpmann. There have been few successful ballet films since. Even *The Turning Point*, which starred Mikhail Baryshnikov, did not use dance to explain the story; it was a story film with ballet sequences put in.

Although film musicals have become bigger and bigger over the years and now rely on the number of dancers they employ as well as spectacular settings, many of the most important images, particularly Fred Astaire in his top hat, white tie and tails, come from the exciting early years of the film musical.

SHALL WE DANCE
Ballet and Theatre Schools

BALLET SCHOOL

There are many different types of ballet school. Firstly there are local schools to which a very young person will go to learn the first steps of dancing, perhaps attending only on Saturday morning each week. This type of school should be chosen with special care as it is very important to get off to a good start with a qualified teacher who knows how to develop young dancers without straining their bodies.

All young dancers want to do all the things they have seen professional dancers do on the stage the moment they join a school. But this is not the right way to start, as young bodies have not yet been completely formed. Young feet with soft bones can be seriously damaged if a girl is allowed to try pointe work too early.

Margot Fonteyn tells the story of one of her first dance schools. When she was very young and travelling with her parents in America, on the way to China, she wanted to do ballet classes in Louisville, Kentucky. They did not know anyone there, so Margot's mother took her to the first ballet school listed in the telephone book. Fortunately she stayed to watch the class, in a studio with a bad floor, that was badly heated and with a teacher who was encouraging the children to do high kicks and splits. They did not do a second class there, fortunately for audiences around the world who have enjoyed Dame Margot's performances since.

The best way to find a good first school is on the recommendation of friends. If this is not possible, the examining bodies in different countries will offer advice. In Britain the Royal Academy of Dancing or the Imperial Society of Teachers of Dancing will supply lists of qualified teachers. These old-established organizations also have teachers worldwide and conduct examinations for teachers in many countries each year.

The specialist dance magazines in Britain and America also carry advertisements for ballet schools and the qualifications of the teachers are always given. It is still advisable to watch a class before making a final decision, as it is possible that a teacher may have qualified a long time ago and is now giving classes which are out of date. Or it is just possible that the personality of the teacher may not suit. Some children like a strict teacher who keeps firm discipline in class. Others may prefer a more relaxed approach. One enjoyable way of finding out how good a school is, is to buy a ticket for their Christmas show (most schools have them). Young people of different levels of learning should be performing numbers to suit their particular talents.

If it is possible to see a class, it is important to notice how good the floor is. It should be non-slip and if possible not just the old floorboards of a church or village hall. The size of the class is also important. If a teacher is packing too many children into a class it will mean that they do not receive the individual attention they need at this early stage in their dance career.

Good music can also help make a good ballet class. For a long time pianists played uninteresting music, usually exercises written specially for ballet class. Today a good pianist will play music which is of the correct tempo, but also something the young dancer might recognize, a pop tune even, and enjoy dancing to. Sometimes a teacher might have to use a tape, which is not as good as live music, but there are now many special tapes which can be found advertised in such magazines as the *Dancing Times*.

The very first classes will not concentrate on steps, but will slowly introduce the young dancer to the rhythm of music and the placing of the body. It will only be after a year or two that they will progress to more disciplined training, possibly following the syllabus of an organization such as the Royal Academy of Dancing. These lead to regular examinations which work up from grade to grade.

There are different syllabuses, or courses, for which you can study and take examinations. The main ones are all based in Britain, all were formed in the 1920s and all arrange examinations all over the world.

In all three courses the Elementary, Intermediate and Advanced syllabuses, known as the major examinations, are of roughly equal standard and are intended for serious students who are thinking of taking up dance as a career. Before these come the 'grades', examinations for younger children, which are much simpler.

The Royal Academy of Dancing was founded in 1920 as the Association of Operatic Dancing, becoming 'Royal' in 1936. It was formed because standards of dance in Britain were very poor, so the editor of the *Dancing Times* asked five leading dancers to form the academy. They represented different schools of dance: Adeline Genée (Danish School), Tamara Karsavina (Russian School), Lucia Cormani (Italian School), Edouard Espinosa (French School) and Phyllis Bedells (English School). It has now grown so important that every year it receives almost 150,000 examination entries from around the world. The

RAD organize the Adeline Genée Gold Medal Awards, which in the past have been won by dancers such as John Gilpin, Doreen Wells, Maria Guerrero, Ravenna Tucker, Roland Price and Leanne Benjamin.

The Cecchetti Society continues the teaching of the great Italian dancer Enrico Cecchetti, who was the ballet master of Diaghilev's company. His style is noted for particularly beautiful *ports de bras*.

The Imperial Society of Teachers of Dancing is the third major examining body. It was founded in 1924 with a very similar basis to the Royal Academy. Apart from classical ballet it covers other forms of dance such as Greek, Scottish, national and modern theatre.

When you have chosen your syllabus, or your teacher has decided which will be best for you, a young dancer will start to take the first simple steps.

First the basic positions of the arms and feet will be taught, as described in the chapter explaining a ballet class. Then the student will be shown how to walk correctly, with stretched toes, making the movements look very delicate. To help this the Royal Academy suggest an exercise called 'Good toes, naughty toes'. You sit on the floor with legs outstretched, back straight. If your feet are turned up, pointing to the ceiling like normal feet, they are 'naughty toes'. You then stretch your feet so that your toes point in the same way as your legs. These are dancers' feet: the 'good toes'.

There will be other exercises, all of which are forming the basis of the steps and positions which will be developed later. Knee bends will soon become full *pliés*; bouncing up and down, stretching knees and pointing feet, will develop into the basis of jumps such as the *entrechat*. And at the end of even these early classes you will learn how to perform a *révérence*, a bow to thank the teacher. If you go on to become a professional dancer you will perform this on stage at the end of a performance.

As you work your way through the grades and pass the examinations you might be giving serious thought to becoming a professional dancer. To do this you will start to look for a different type of school.

◼ *One Step On*

Some young dancers will leave their normal school and enter a specialist ballet school, often a boarding-school, around the age of eleven. Others are able to continue their academic schooling at their normal school while taking their ballet classes under the guidance of an organization such as the Royal Academy or the Cecchetti Society. These dancers will usually join a full-time ballet school as soon as they finish their academic schooling at around the age of sixteen.

If you choose to attend a ballet school as a boarder, you will be doing so because you are very keen to become a professional dancer. Life at these schools is harder than at a normal school. Day starts much earlier, but you will hear few grumbles as all the pupils really want to be there. This is not like other schools where pupils arrive late and yawn through the first few classes. In a ballet school everyone is keen and bright even though the day can start as early as 7.15, when the rising bell rings.

A school such as the junior school of the Royal Ballet expects hundreds of youngsters to apply for entry each year. The school only accepts about twenty pupils, aged eleven, each year. Those lucky children have to do more than just dance. They will have attended preliminary auditions and then the final auditions, when the panel of teachers decide who they will accept on the basis of musicality, personality and physical suitability.

These days the medical examination can play a great part in deciding a young dancer's future. With such competition for a few precious places at the important schools they do not want to waste a place on a dancer who is obviously going to grow too tall, for instance. Medical science can now predict within a couple of inches how tall a child will grow. At the time it may seem very cruel to a child to be rejected, but it may save them much unhappiness in later life if things do not work out as they hoped in their dancing career.

Junior school will normally last for five years, much the same length of time as at an academic school, before graduation into the Upper School.

After breakfast, which you will all take together, the whole school breaks up into classes according to which year you are studying in. The younger dancers will get their school books ready. They will have classes just as they would do if they were at a normal school, covering many of the same subjects, although they usually have more music lessons. Though they don't have to play an instrument, most do. You will not be pressed hard to be academically brilliant, but a young dancer should have a good knowledge of literature and languages, as well as simple science and geography. With so much energy going into the dancing it is not surprising that many young dancers don't shine brilliantly at other subjects, but in most ballet schools they are lucky to have a little extra attention, as the classes are often smaller than at other schools.

The older pupils, in the fourth and fifth years, will go for their shoes, to be ready for their first ballet class which might well start before 9. This means that they have to be ready and doing warming-up exercises well before this time.

Boys and girls take separate classes and keep their teachers for a year at a time. This is essential so that the teacher can follow the progress of a pupil, as not all dancers develop at exactly the same rate even though they are in the same class.

Not long ago a school might consist almost entirely of girls, but recently many more boys have joined and almost one-third of the pupils at Royal Ballet School are boys. There are even more in theatre schools that teach subjects other than dancing. The London Studio Centre in London and the School for the Performing Arts (which the school in *Fame* was modelled on) in New York are good examples.

The boys will have classical ballet classes, but they will also have periods for gymnastics and weight-training to build up their muscles. They cannot lift a ballerina by classical technique alone!

Apart from academic work and ballet classes, the day will also be filled with character classes to learn national dances, which appear in ballets such as *Swan Lake*. There will be the occasional jazz class and a modern class, as today's dancers have to be flexible and able to dance in many styles. Character dancing will be practised and there will be classes in the art of mime. Time may also have to be found to rehearse a ballet which is actually going to be performed on stage, as it is important to get as much stage experience as possible. This in turn means that you will be given lessons in the art of stage make-up, usually by a dancer from the company. This all makes for a very full day!

Throughout your time in ballet school, the teachers will always be assessing your progress. Sadly, promising pupils at the age of eleven can develop in unexpected ways and find that by the time they are thirteen they are no longer suitable, for reasons to do with their physique or their dancing. They have to leave. This is one reason why it is important to continue with academic training while dancing. It is then easier to go back to an academic school.

Life in ballet can produce more disappointments than almost any other career. If you succeed in graduating out of the junior school into the senior school, it is still possible that your dream of entering the Royal Ballet or another major company will not come true. There are only a few places available each year and there may be too many really good dancers to fill them. It may be that although you are a very good dancer you are not exactly the type a company is looking for. Companies have their own style and like to employ dancers who fit into it. The New York City Ballet, for instance, likes girls with short bodies, small heads and long legs. If you are not this shape your chances of getting in are very small.

But do not let this put you off doing your personal best, achieving as much as you can from your ballet-school training. Apart from teaching you how to dance it will also give you poise and confidence, which are always a help in later life.

■ GREAT SCHOOLS

■ *The Paris Opéra Ballet School*

This is the oldest ballet school in the world and it is from here that many of the basics of teaching were formed. King Louis XIV of France founded the Paris Opéra in

1669. The school was founded in 1713 and the greatest of dancers have taught there, including Marie Taglioni, the original Sylphide. During the last half of the nineteenth century it lost its prominent place, but it started to regain its importance in the 1930s. In the Paris Opéra examinations continue after the dancers leave school, and promotion in the company depends on them, from *corps de ballet* to *quadrille*, to *coryphée*, to *sujets*, and then *premier danseur* or *première danseuse*. At the top come the *étoiles*. Only in very recent years have there been exceptions to these rules where dancers have not had to climb up through all the ranks.

■ The Royal Danish Ballet School

The Royal Danish Ballet is one of the oldest companies in the world, having been started in 1748. The school associated with the company is now well over two hundred years old. Children from the school have always been regarded as part of the big theatre family and many of them appear on the stage while still tiny, especially in ballets by the great Danish choreographer Auguste Bournonville. They may just stand and wave on the bridge at the back of the stage in *Napoli*, or they may dance Scottish reels in *La Sylphide*. Many of the children who enter the school then spend most of their lives in the Royal Theatre, as pupils, then as dancers and then teachers. Some have become directors of the company. Many of the dancers trained at the Royal Danish Ballet School are now to be seen with other companies. In London Peter Schaufuss is Artistic Director of London Festival Ballet. He made one of his earliest appearances at the age of six as Peter the Page in Frederick Ashton's *Romeo and Juliet*.

His mother, Mona Vangsaae, was Juliet. His father, Frank Schaufuss, was Mercutio. In New York Peter Martins is Associate Ballet Master of the New York City Ballet and, in turn, his son Nilas has already graduated from the school.

The Kirov School

This school carries on the tradition of the Tsar of Russia's Imperial Ballet School, which trained the great dancers at the end of the last century including Vaslav Nijinsky, Tamara Karsavina and Anna Pavlova. Karsavina tells the story of her life in the school in her book *Theatre Street*, called after the address of the school. After the Russian Revolution of 1917 the authorities did not want classical ballet to continue, as it reminded them of the great days of the tsar's court, but the great ballerina and teacher Agrippina Vaganova convinced the Commissar for Culture that the school and the company should continue. Most of the great Russian ballerinas were taught by her, including Galina Ulanova and Irina Kolpakova. Other pupils of the school have included Yuri Soloviev, Rudolf Nureyev, Mikhail Baryshnikov and Natalia Makarova. The school was named after Vaganova in 1956.

The Royal Ballet School

The Royal Ballet itself grew out of the school which Dame Ninette de Valois founded in London when she left the Diaghilev ballet in 1926. She started by producing dances for Lilian Baylis who ran the Old Vic Theatre and later Sadler's Wells Theatre. She moved her school into

Sadler's Wells and it remained there throughout the early years of British ballet. One of her earliest pupils was Margot Fonteyn, who joined at the age of fourteen and soon after became the ballerina of the company when Alicia Markova left. It became the Royal Ballet School in 1956 after the company had been awarded a Royal Charter, and today has a junior, boarding-school at White Lodge, Richmond, Surrey, once a royal hunting lodge, and an upper school at Barons Court, London. With a few exceptions all the dancers of the Royal Ballet from corps de ballet to ballerina were trained at the school, as are many dancers in other companies in Britain and across Europe.

The school has always had many foreign students, and these have included John Neumeier, who now directs the ballet in Hamburg, and Jiri Kylián, who directs the Nederlands Dans Theater and whose ballets have been danced by the Royal Ballet. The school is now directed by the Royal Ballet ballerina, Dame Merle Park.

■ The School of American Ballet

This is the official school of New York City Ballet and, with few exceptions, it trains most of the dancers who join the company. It was started in 1933 when George Balanchine left Europe for America. Some ballets which Balanchine created for his students are still danced by the company, including *Serenade*. Balanchine trained the dancers in exactly the way he wanted, and from this has grown the style of American ballet. The school is now housed in the Juilliard School of Music, just a short walk from the company's home at the State Theater in Lincoln Center, New York. The teachers include Stanley

Williams, a Danish teacher who has trained many fine male dancers. There are also famous Russian ballerinas such as Alexandra Danilova, who still teaches at the age of eighty-three. She played the part of the ballet mistress in the film *The Turning Point*.

Many of the other major companies have important ballet schools. In Canada, the School of the National Ballet of Canada under Betty Oliphant has trained fine young dancers and the Australian Ballet School produces strong dancers. From the Royal Swedish Ballet School have come many marvellous male dancers, who can be seen in companies such as London Festival Ballet and American Ballet Theater, both of which have schools of their own.

■ THEATRE SCHOOL

Dance of all types is taught at theatre schools. These are for training students for every branch of the theatre: dancing in shows, commercials, videos and ballet companies, playing in orchestras or acting and directing. At the same time many give a full academic education.

Life in these schools is a mixture of the hard work of the classroom and studio and the excitement of the professional theatre, as many students find jobs while they are still in the school.

Some take children as early as eight or nine years old, but most settle for around twelve or thirteen. Others only take pupils after they have finished their basic full-time education, around the age of fifteen or sixteen.

In Britain a typical school of the last kind is the London Studio Centre, with its handsome new studios near the centre of the city, which were opened in 1987. Founded by Bridget Espinosa in 1978, when it had just one studio, it now has eleven ballet studios, three music rooms, four drama studios, two rehearsal rooms, together with a library, a canteen, a body-control studio and a physio-therapy room. It is one of the most impressive in the country. Its Patron is Dame Ninette de Valois, founder of the Royal Ballet, and Dame Alicia Markova gives lectures and private coaching to the graduate class of students who wish to join a classical ballet company.

The school has 350 pupils and a teaching staff of almost fifty to cope with them. The subjects studied range from classical ballet to modern dance, musical staging, mime, ballet history (for a state examination) and radio and television technique. The pupils' timetable can also be arranged to allow them to take advanced academic education if they want to.

Requests for the school's prospectus come in at a rate of around fifty a week from schools, careers advisers or parents. About 500 young people apply for places each year. Biddie Espinosa (as she is known throughout the ballet world) and her teachers take auditions nearly every Monday to choose the lucky ones who will be offered a place.

Students come from all over Britain, as well as abroad. Many of the British students are paid for by the local government of their home area, just like university students, as the school is accredited by the Council for Dance Education and Training. Others succeed at the auditions for one of the several scholarships the school offers in honour of distinguished people in the world of theatre, such as Sir Anton Dolin and Dame Anna Neagle, an award sponsored by Cameron Mackintosh, the pro-ducer of many great musicals shows, including *Cats*.

When these young people come to London they are

Students at the London Studio Centre performing in their annual summer show.

given some help with accommodation, but most find that they have to work hard in the evenings to help pay for it. They find themselves selling programmes in theatres, putting together cabaret acts for pubs or working as extras in films or television. Some of this is well-paid and it is all valuable experience for a future in the entertainment business, whether in ballet or show-business.

The timetable you would follow if you had a place in this school would be made up to suit you individually. It would take into account what training in classical ballet or other subjects you had before you arrived at the school. Your main classes would be filled in and then room would be found for other subjects. Young dancers have to be versatile today and so you would take classes in modern dance, mime and even fencing. There are singing lessons three times a week, as well as voice coaching. And those specializing in acting will also take dance lessons, as actors today have to be able to use their bodies expressively. Theatre companies such as the Royal Shakespeare Company or the National Theatre, which once only produced classic plays, now put on modern musicals and many experimental plays.

This excellent system of individual timetables takes a computer to work it all out. But it means that you can progress at your own speed and won't feel frustrated at being in a first-year class for no better reason than that it is your first year at the school. If your teacher thinks you have the talent you can be switched to a second-year class at the press of a button! It also means that students from all years mix together, which creates a good atmosphere in the school.

There is also the chance to mix with, and watch, professional dancers at work. A major choreographer like Sir Kenneth MacMillan might be creating a ballet for a small group in one studio, a television choreographer might be rehearsing a routine in another. In the body-control studio an ice-skater like John Curry might be keeping himself in shape, while the London City Ballet, which has made the school its base, might be working on its repertoire.

This enterprising company teaches its ballets to students and, when the occasion arises, uses them to replace injured dancers or when a larger corps de ballet is needed. All good experience.

Every year you would have to prepare a short piece of your own choice – classical dance, jazz dance, acting or singing – for the annual assessments. Time is allowed in an already busy timetable for you to prepare it; you would have to make sure it was also properly costumed.

You will then perform your piece before a panel of teachers from the school, joined by well-known people from the theatre world. They might include a famous ballet dancer or company director, a musical director from a West End show or a theatre director.

Each student is given a thorough assessment of the work and various diplomas and prizes are awarded. The best of the assessments are then given extra perform-ances for an audience of friends, dance and theatre critics and other guests. Many young dancers have been spot-ted by choreographers at performances like these and offered parts in shows on the stage or on television. They take them eagerly as, apart from the welcome extra income, it is still possible for them to continue with their training at the school during the day while performing in the evenings.

Students do drop out of the three-year course, but they are surprisingly few; perhaps only two or three because of poor performance. It is more likely that a few will leave through problems of discipline, such as not turning up for class regularly, for instance. Though life at a school like this can look free and easy, it is in fact as regulated as at any other. Students sign in in the morning and out after their last class, with roll-calls just like any other school. Biddie Espinosa likes to avoid losing students this way and finds that often a good hard look at their timetable and a talk about what they *really* want to do can get them working well again.

The school puts on two shows a year: a summer revue with each class contributing a ballet, a jazz routine or a dramatic piece, and a full-scale musical at Christmas.

Students do not automatically have a part in the show, but have to audition and prove their worth. Some never make it into the big shows, but all appear at some time, often in one of the eight plays that are put on each year.

The show is produced in a large theatre to professional standards: there's a full orchestra, excellent decor and lighting and packed houses. The musical chosen (and they have ranged from *Carousel* to *Cabaret* to *Chicago*) gives as many students as possible a chance to shine. They not only give their friends and families a good show, but also gain invaluable experience themselves.

Whatever the merits of the London Studio Centre the most famous theatre school has to be the High School for the Performing Arts in New York. It became well-known through the movie and the television series *Fame*, which gave a misleading impression of what life there is really like. In fact, the school would not let the television company make the series in their building as they were sure it would not show the true picture.

As a student at the school says, 'The series got it all wrong. First of all, it made it look as though every student can sing, dance, act and play a musical instrument all equally brilliantly. It's just not like that. We specialize, just like any other school. We may be pretty good at our own subject, but we don't even try a lot of the others. The day just wouldn't be long enough to do what all those kids in *Fame* did.'

A school for students specially interested in the performing arts was opened by Mayor La Guardia of New York in 1936. He thought that as there were schools for people who wanted to specialize in engineering or other practical subjects, there should also be a school for children who wanted to specialize in the theatre arts.

A few years later another public school (in America this means just that, a school open to anyone who lives in the area) was opened in midtown New York near Times Square, the theatre centre of the city. This was the School for the Performing Arts and it is about to celebrate its fortieth birthday.

Entry to the school is tough. As a teacher says, 'Every year we get two thousand or more children applying to get in. We have to be hard on them, because we only take about sixty-five each year. I have to talk to all the children before they go through their auditions. Usually children are honest at this age, around twelve. I ask them what they want to do when they grow up. You'd be surprised at some of the answers I get. One little girl wanted to be an engineer. So I asked what she was doing trying to get into our school. Because her mother wanted her to, was her answer. I just had to turn her down. Better she is disappointed now than in a few years' time. I have to turn down lots of other kids who think they should be in here. Some come after years of training and I know they just won't fit. Others have had little training, but we can see that there is a talent which we would like to develop.'

But most have started early, too early, some think.

Ballet class in the film Fame set in New York's High School for the Performing Arts.

After three years at the school one girl says, 'I started dancing at the age of four in pre-ballet classes. Then I graduated to ballet class and I have done nothing else since. I think this is too young. I have seen lots of really great kids burn themselves out by twelve. Twelve, just think of it. I was afraid that would happen to me, but I got over it. But there was a lot of pressure round that age.'

The teachers taking the auditions have to be tough, as the life children will be letting themselves in for is hard. There will be a minimum of three hours' dance class each day for dance students, as well as lots of other activities related to the theatre, before they start on the academic work which plays an important part in the educational programme.

There are other problems to cope with as well. Eating can be a big one, as a teacher explains, 'Girls come into the school looking like wisps at twelve, but within a year or two they start developing and it shows around the hips, not through eating too much, just the natural development of the body. They have to keep to a strict regime, which can be tough. It's a problem to get it right. They are using so much energy in the day, but can get the balance wrong and not burn off all they eat. Specially junk food. But I have to be straight and tell them if they look too heavy. They'll never make it if they are.'

Young students appear very grown up in this world. Young people of thirteen and fourteen can talk about the business as though they were adult. Says one: 'I always wanted to dance, and I like what I'm doing. But hardly a day goes by without me thinking that I'd like to try something else. That's why I'm pretty serious about my school classes. I know that if I stay in dancing my life is going to be like a gypsy moving from job to job or apartment to apartment. I guess I'll stick it out as I do get a kick out of pirouetting better than I could a few weeks ago or jumping higher. Underneath I know that I want to be recognized. Hell, I know I want to be Baryshnikov!'

But there aren't that many Baryshnikovs. Most of the young dancers at the school settle down just to learn and worry about work prospects when the chance comes. Another student says, 'Some of my friends have already been offered contracts, and we are still only in the fourth year. I haven't, but the Boston Ballet has invited me to spend summer with them and if things go right I may be offered a job as an apprentice in their second company.' This is the realistic approach. This young man realizes that overnight fame comes only to the few.

When the end-of-year show is put on, usually a big musical like *Follies* by Stephen Sondheim, there are hours of extra work, as the show is produced, like those of the London Studio Centre, to top professional standards. Says the producer, 'This is the most difficult time for our kids. After a full day they rehearse and rehearse and then have to stay even later while I give notes (corrections). It's the time that tests their stamina, their technique and their attitude at the end of four years' hard work. Some years I don't think we've made a great job, especially when we get prima donnas going off in fits of tears three or four times a week during rehearsals. Whether the kids are going into musicals or ballet companies, they're going to have to face up to a tough world outside of here. Putting on a show like this really warns them what life is going to be like.'

The same teacher also believes that working on a show, in the corps de ballet or in the orchestra (the school has four full orchestras, three string groups and a jazz orchestra!) helps the students learn how to work in a team. They may shine by themselves for a moment, but they have to support everyone else in the group.

It's a great thing to get into the show, but not everyone does. If a dancer has missed too many classes, even because of illness or injury, they are counted out. It's not only great because it's fun to perform, but it may also help start a career.

Important choreographers, musical directors and agents are invited and a young dancer may be spotted and put into a show. Their teachers encourage this, as these chances don't come round that often. 'I always say, take it, kid. Make good money for a year or two if the show runs. Meet experienced people in the theatre and benefit from them. You can always go to college later, at twenty-four or twenty-five. In fact, in America, I think college professors like older, mature students. If this is why they came to the school, they should go out there and get it. They tell me they *want* their name in lights or on the cover of *People* magazine. They tell me they *want* to be a star. *Wanting* is a useless word. They have to get out there and do it. Sweat for it. That's the only way and that's how we try to teach them here.'

Since these interviews were given the grand old building which housed the School for the Performing Arts is no longer a landmark of New York. Early in 1988 it burned down. No other building will ever have the same theatrical atmosphere, but the good work of the school will continue elsewhere.

I WON'T DANCE, DON'T ASK ME
A Dancer's Life

When a young dancer graduates from a ballet or theatre school their first problem is to find a job. The major companies such as the Royal Ballet or the New York City Ballet have only a few places available for new dancers each year, which means that the very best pupils in the schools which belong to these companies (the Royal Ballet School and the School of American Ballet) will already have been offered a place in the corps de ballet or, in very special cases, as a junior soloist. But the rest will have to start going to auditions for smaller companies both at home and, more often, abroad.

For a young dancer in Britain this will most probably mean setting out early in the year for a long journey across Europe, auditioning for the dozens of small opera houses, particularly those in Germany. In America, pupils at New York's School of American Ballet and other schools will audition for one of the many regional companies based in cities across the country.

Ballet auditions are very straightforward. The company teacher will give a class, which will be watched by the company director. He will make a fairly quick decision as to who he wants to keep behind to do a few more complicated exercises, or perhaps he will ask them to learn a short piece of choreography. And then he chooses. This sounds simple, but it is a difficult time for the dancers, who, through nerves, will often feel that they have not done their best.

Not every young dancer wants to work in one of the big companies. Some might deliberately look for a place in a small company. This could well give them greater opportunities to work with choreographers they admire or to dance important roles much earlier than they could hope to if they were just a corps de ballet member of an opera-house company.

But life will be much the same whichever company a young ballet dancer succeeds in joining. It will not be that much different to life during the last months of training at ballet school, except for the knowledge that there will be a performance at the end of many working days.

For every dancer, from the newest member of the corps de ballet to the big stars of the ballet, the day will start the same. The daily class is the most important part of every dancer's life. The young dancer will need it to build on the technique learned at school, while the stars, especially when they get older, have to look after their bodies very carefully.

In class, all dancers are equal, but young dancers can learn not only from what the teacher tells them, but also from working alongside the principal dancers and soloists, watching their methods. Every day the great dancer who, only the night before was being showered with flowers and receiving tumultuous applause, once again becomes a student. They dress in the same simple practice clothes as the young dancers and receive the same corrections from the teacher.

Daily class will vary in length according to the amount of other work which has to be fitted in to a full day. By the standards of other professions the dancer has a long day, but like other groups of workers they have a trade union, called Equity in Britain and America, which will have negotiated just how many hours they will be expected to work. They will have agreed the pay as well. The total number of hours the dancer is allowed to work each day will have to allow time for all sorts of activities. This might mean that on a day when there is a performance, which could last up to three hours, there is not much time for anything else.

In Britain and America dancers work longer than in some other countries. For example, in Sweden the dancers of the Royal Swedish Ballet have rules so strict that on performance days there is hardly time for anything else other than a short class. But so important is class that it will never be cut down to less than an hour. To do so would harm the dancers in the long run and this would show during the performances. Cutting class down too much could also cause injuries to bodies which have not been trained properly. It is essential that the dancers warm up all their muscles before starting a hard day's work.

The details of the day's work will be on the call-sheet on the notice board. For some the day may be free, for others it may mean dancing all day. For the really unfortunate it might mean a few short rehearsals with lots of time to kill in between. As it is not wise for the dancer, once the body is warm, to leave the studio, this can be frustrating. It is tempting to leave to go shopping, but this would mean doing a short warm-up barre on returning, or otherwise risk injury. It is much better to spend the time knitting tights or just watching and learning as others work.

Although the rehearsals which take place can look the same to an outsider, they have very different characters depending on the type of ballet being rehearsed. If the company is putting on a big classic ballet which they have performed before, such as *Swan Lake* or *The Sleeping Beauty*, the rehearsal is to remind dancers of the steps and to introduce new dancers to the production. This can mean repeating the same scenes over and over again until the ballet master is happy with the result.

While the leading dancers are rehearsing, a junior company member might be expected to dance alone at the back of the studio, learning the basic steps for themselves. This way they will already have a good idea of both the ballet and the steps if they are suddenly thrown onto the stage when someone else is sick or injured. Dancers have to be self-reliant and show some initiative in this way.

The other type of rehearsal, that for a new work, is much more interesting for the dancer. To work with great choreographers when they are creating a completely new ballet is a challenge, as a well-trained intelligent dancer can help the choreographer in so many ways. First, of course, there is the dancer's well-trained body which should be capable of doing whatever steps the choreographer wants. Just as a musician prefers to play on a special instrument, so choreographers like to work with well-trained dancers.

A dancer with a special technique might even inspire the choreographer to create some new, unusual steps or poses. In this way the dancer becomes part of the ballet and is not just a body being twisted about like a doll by the choreographer. A special personality might inspire the choreographer to create a different type of character, just as Margot Fonteyn inspired Frederick Ashton and Lynn Seymour inspired Kenneth MacMillan.

Not all of the day will be taken up dancing. If a new production is being created there might be long, boring sessions for costume fittings. The costume designer might make endless alterations while the costume is on the dancer and the dancers themselves will want to make sure that they can move freely in it. In the case of many modern ballets it is quite possible that the designer will paint patterns directly onto tights while the dancer is wearing them. Girls have the additional problem of making sure that the hair styles are possible to do in the time available during the performance. In a three-act ballet, such as *Swan Lake*, the girls of the corps de ballet may have to be peasants in one act, with flowers in their hair, and then be swan maidens in the second act. This allows them only the length of the interval to change not only their dresses and shoes, but also put their hair into the classical style, perhaps with a swan headdress. In the following interval they will have to change into ornate costumes to appear as court ladies or the national dancers in the third, Black Swan, act. And then they have to become swan maidens, yet again, for the last lakeside scene!

Dress rehearsals of new ballets give the dancer the chance to work out their costume and hair changes. This is also the time when dancers may have to pose for publicity photographs in different costumes, usually getting cold while the photographer is occupied with the technical details of taking the pictures. They might then be asked to repeat the same jump time after time until the photographer gets it just right.

Preparation for the evening performance can start a couple of hours before curtain-up; for each dancer it is different. Some have bodies which do not need much warming up, their muscles work easily the whole time. Others will need the short warm-up exercises which will be given on stage. Before this time suitable make-up will have been put on. For some roles this can take an hour or more, especially for characters such as Dr Coppélius in *Coppélia* or the evil magician Kotschei in *The Firebird*, both of which need false noses, which are built up with putty, and elaborate wigs and moustaches.

For ballerinas this is the time to choose shoes for the performance from the dozens of pairs they have. They will have been prepared earlier, with ribbons sewn on and toes sewn with small tight stitches to make them last longer and to make slipping less likely. Some pointe shoes are better for some roles than others, which means that the ballerina dancing Odette and Odile in *Swan Lake* may wear at least three pairs during a complete perform-ance. Some dancers like very soft shoes with little sup-port, others like a firm shoe. It is a very personal choice.

After the warm-up the dancers' make-up might need retouching and hair given a final spray before they put on their costume and are ready for the performance. There are always last-minute repairs to be done – a ribbon that has come loose, a fastener that won't close – which might mean a quick visit to the wardrobe department. Careful dancers will make sure that any props they are going to need are in their correct place and that doors or windows open properly. Dame Alicia Markova remembers one occasion when before a performance of *Giselle* a careful stagehand nailed up the door of her house, to stop it swinging open. When she heard the music for her en-trance she pulled on the door – which wouldn't move. She had to run around the house and appear through the garden gate.

This may also be the time for a dancer to practise some particularly difficult step or complicated partnering. A ballerina dancing the role of Aurora in *The Sleeping Beauty* might take this opportunity to practise the balances of the *Rose Adagio* with her four princes. It may also give a last opportunity for a dancer to have a word with the conductor about the speed a particular solo should be played.

Over the loudspeakers backstage the call comes for the dancers who open the ballet and from the orchestra pit comes the sound of the orchestra tuning up. There is also the sound of chatter as the theatre fills up.

On stage everyone is ready under the harsh lights which will soon change to suit the ballet. There is the sound of applause as the conductor enters the orchestra pit; a hush as the lights dim and the overture starts. When it ends, applause, and then with a swish the great curtain sweeps up and the front-of-house lights blind the dancers for a moment.

There is no sign of the hard day's work which has gone into the making of the performance. The prince lifts his ballerina without any of the effort he was allowed to show in class, the ballerina looks for a light out front for her to 'spot' on when she is doing her sparkling *fouettés*, the corps de ballet are looking out of the corner of their eyes, trying to keep in straight lines without making it too obvious. The last-minute replacement is trying to look happy in someone else's enormous costume and the conductor has got the tempo all wrong. But none of this must show as the audience enjoys a magic evening at the ballet.

As the performance ends, the excitement of the audience erupts with wild applause and a shower of flowers. There are endless curtain calls for the whole company, a special cheer for the last-minute stand-in. The curtain comes down for the final time and there is a rush backstage to dressing rooms and showers. Perhaps there's a reception or a party for the dancers, if it is a first performance. More likely they hurry into street clothes and push their way through a crowd at the stage door, eager to get home. For whatever the excitement of the night the one thing all dancers know for sure is that first thing next morning they will once more be in practice clothes ready to start their daily class . . .

Not all classically trained dancers join ballet companies, some by their own choice, others because too many dancers graduate each year and it is impossible to find work. Many of these find their way into dancing on television or on the stage in musicals.

For these dancers auditions are usually much more terrible things. And they have to do so many of them, as a job may last only a few days.

For big shows literally hundreds of dancers can turn up for an audition, knowing that perhaps ten people at most will be chosen. At a good audition the choreographer will allow only a few people and give them a good chance to show what they can do. At bad auditions dancers are crammed into a studio, given a few basic steps and then told that they are not going to be used.

How a dancer looks is just as important in these auditions as dance talent. The dancer also has to look the type the choreographer prefers. It can be a sad time especially as it may be well-known that the choreographers are going to choose dancers they have worked with before, but feel obliged to hold an open audition. Dancers at auditions have to be quick at picking up steps, as the choreographer is sure to set a routine and want it repeated almost immediately.

After the first routine a few names will be called out and asked to stay. A quick thank-you-for-coming dismisses the rest. And even this is not the end of it. The choreographer will set more complicated routines for the dancers to do individually. There may then be an interview to test the dancer's voice and a few test Polaroid or video shots will be taken if the audition is for a television or a pop video.

If the dancers are lucky they will be told there and then if they have been successful. But there may be a terrible wait for a few days before a telephone call tells them if they have been successful or not.

Once in a show the dancers' day is not as controlled by timetables as that of dancers in ballet companies. This means that they have to have the discipline to organize their own lives if they want to keep their bodies in shape and their dancing up to the mark. If a dancer succeeds at an audition and is given a part in a musical, daily class will be given during the rehearsal period. But once the show has started its run of performances it is more likely that classes will only be given when rehearsals are called to keep the show fresh or introduce new members of the cast.

Responsibility for these rehearsals will be that of the 'Dance Captain', the equivalent of the ballet master. But their responsibility is only regarding work that goes into the show. They are not responsible for helping the dancer keep up the over-all standard of work. The class they give would probably only involve a jazz class to get the dancer's body moving, not one concerned with the improvement of technique. To do this dancers in music-als or television must make their own arrangements for class. They must find out which teachers are giving 'open' classes which anyone can attend, and then they must have the self-discipline to attend regularly. Unlike the dancers with ballet companies, they have to pay for their own classes. In addition to basic ballet classes to improve their technique, they may also have to pay for specialist classes in jazz, tap or modern dance as it is extremely important for those working in the commercial theatre to have a wide range of dance ability. It is also advisable for them to take singing lessons as well.

Dancers have been called the work-horses of the theatre. Physically it is very tiring and the effort which goes into keeping in shape can never stop. Their day is always full, from early morning to late at night. They can spend many boring hours standing on stage without dancing and they can spend even more boring times in rehearsal rooms. They have little chance to meet anyone outside the dance world. They work with each other day in, day out. This can lead to times of stress and tension, shouting and arguments. But as dancers are all good at playing pranks and mimicking each other, these moments of drama soon blow away in gales of laughter.

I CAN DO THAT
Ballet, Modern, Jazz and Tap Classes

Young people take up dancing for many different reasons. Many girls have seen ballet and think it looks pretty and attractive. Many boys have seen ballet and don't want to do it at all, preferring some sort of sport.

The opening song of the musical *A Chorus Line* is 'I can do that'. It is sung by a boy who goes along to dance class with his sister. He decides he can do it as well as she can. This has happened in real life to people now very famous, such as Anthony Dowell, Director of the Royal Ballet. In the past it was not very common for boys to take up ballet, even though it is as physical as any sport. But today, when there is so much dancing on the stage and on television, many more boys go to ballet, jazz or tap classes. For some it is just good fun. But for others it can be the start of a career on the ballet stage, in a musical or on television.

■BALLET CLASS

The basis of all good dancing is the daily ballet class, which all dancers do every day, long after they have left their ballet schools. Dancers, no matter how famous, remain students until the end of their dancing lives. In fact, the older they become the more important the daily class is to keep their technique up to standard.

The daily class is not only for learning, it is also

important for the self-discipline all dancers must have. When they are in school their teachers tell them what to do and there is a set programme to follow every day. But as soon as they join a ballet company or, even worse, have to spend some time looking for a place in a company, the self-discipline of the class becomes very important. You have to make sure yourself that all your ballet gear is in good shape and that you go to class every day.

Ballet class has developed over three centuries from the first steps in the Royal Academy of the Dance in Paris in 1661 when the teacher Beauchamp first wrote down the basic positions of the feet. He did not invent them, he just brought together the ideas of the time, which were developments of the formal walking and skipping which took place in court ballets. Technique has developed incredibly since then, but the positions from which all other ballet steps start and end have remained almost the same.

The main difference is that as technique developed the importance of proper turn-out was recognized. The legs must be turned-out from the hips, and not from the knees or by straining the ankles. There is a very obvious reason for turn-out at the hip. Can you imagine a stage performance in which the leg could only move like that of an average person – up and down to the front, like marching? Turn-out means that the dancer can face the audience and move his or her leg out to the side in a graceful arc.

It is impossible to learn to dance from reading a book. It is also dangerous to try one of the more complicated steps from a description. The guidance of a good teacher in a studio is essential. However, a few notes to explain what certain steps are can be a helpful reminder in between classes.

The five positions of the feet and their related arm positions (which can vary slightly, depending on which syllabus the dancer is studying) are the basis of every move a dancer does.

In *First Position* the legs are together and the heels are touching, with the feet forming a straight line, the toes pointing outwards, away from each other. When in this position the dancer should stand straight with the body raised from the hips, breathing from the diaphragm to fill the lungs well.

In *Second Position* the feet are apart by about one and a half times the length of the dancer's foot, with the weight of the body balanced evenly above them.

The five positions.

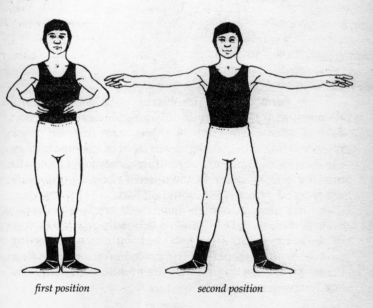

first position   *second position*

third position   *fourth position*

Third Position is an important position for young dancers, as it is halfway to learning the very important *Fifth Position*. The dancer's feet are brought back together, but with one slightly in front of the other. They are then crossed just enough for the heel of one foot to fit into the hollow instep of the other. In other words they are crossed parallel just about half way.

For the next, *Fourth Position*, there are two versions; open and crossed. In the open position the feet are almost in the same position as first, but with one foot about twelve inches in front of the other. In the crossed position the feet will be as though they are in fifth, but again with one foot well in front of the other.

fifth position

Fifth Position is the most difficult for a young dancer to achieve, unless they are born with natural turn-out. Work to achieve this will be gradual, going through third position until the feet can be positioned parallel, with the heel of one foot against the toe of the other. This position needs the greatest possible turn-out and should not be forced.

Each position of the feet has a corresponding position of the arms, called the *ports de bras*. The arms should always be relaxed with the line of the arm continuing through to the tip of the middle finger. No ugly bent elbows. The position from which all other positions start is called *bras bas*, meaning low arms or arms down. The arms are held a little in front of the body, dropping naturally in a curve, a little rounded at the elbow. The fingers continue the curve to make an oval shape.

In some teaching methods this is called *first position*, but in others it is the starting position before going into first position. The arms are in the same position, but held out in front of the body instead of hanging down. For *Second Position* the arms swing out to be stretched out at the sides of the body, sloping a little naturally from the shoulders, the palms showing to the front and the elbows not dropping.

In *Third Position* one arm will remain outstretched as in

99

second position, but the other curves forward out front as in first position.

To go into *Fourth Position* one arm remains out in second while the other is raised over the head in a natural curve, just ever so slightly out in front of the head.

When the outstretched arm is raised to match the raised one, the arms are in *Fifth Position*. The shoulders are relaxed and do not stretch up; the hands are a few inches apart. Sometimes this position is called *au couronne*.

The way the shoulders are held is called *épaulement*. Good bearing is very important, and the head must always be held in a natural position, to match the rest of the pose.

■ Working Through a Ballet Class

The basic ballet class always follows the same routine, only the steps change each day to avoid boredom, especially for the exercises during the second part of the class, centre work. Some teachers may make small changes in the running order of the exercises, but this is not important.

Before class a conscientious dancer will have done some exercises alone to warm up the muscles ready for the class. Working directly into class with cold muscles can cause cramps or injuries, even though the class itself is made in such way that the muscles warm up gradually. Sometimes dancers wear woolly leg-warmers during the early part of the class. These look good on stage or television, but it is best if they can be avoided as the teacher should be able to see the students' feet and legs clearly to give corrections.

demi plié

plié

Class starts with exercises at the barre, a wooden rail at roughly waist height on the studio wall. The dancer's hand should lightly rest on it. It is not there to be gripped tightly and give a false sense of balance.

The exercises given at the barre all are done 'both sides', which means that first they are done on one supporting leg, and then on the other, to give equally balanced training to both sides.

Work starts with *pliés*, supported by lightly holding the barre. They are called *pliés* after the French for 'bend', as they are a movement in which the body is slowly lowered by bending the knees. They help strengthen the legs ready for the exercises to come and also improve turn-out. The back is kept straight and the hips level. And your bottom must not stick out! The movement up and down has to be very smooth, with the heels kept on the floor in second position, but allowed to rise as necessary when doing them in first, third and fifth positions.

The *pliés* are followed by *tendus*, an exercise to stretch the leg and foot from a closed position to an open position, with the toe never leaving the floor. This helps develop fast footwork for the later allegro (fast) exercises. The *glissées* take this a step further, the foot and leg gliding (which is what glissée means) but this time the toe can leave the floor by about two inches. The foot should be nicely pointed.

The class moves on to *ronds de jambes à terre*, in which the legs are worked in a circular action rather than just back and to. The working leg (the moving one) draws a semi-circle on the floor, the movement coming from the hip.

Now that the legs are getting warmer they can move more freely in the *battements frappés*. They are fast, sharp movements as the leg swings, not in a complete arc, back and front, but from a closed position to an open one and back again. *Frapper* means 'to strike', and this describes how the movement feels.

Fondus are another step towards raising the foot high off the ground (up to now the foot has only been a few inches away from it) and warms the muscles up more. The basic exercise consists of raising one leg forwards while doing a slow *demi-plié* at the same time. One leg will be carrying the whole weight of the body for the first time. As the name suggests, this exercise has to be done smoothly and slowly. It will help the take off for jumps later in the class and make the landings soft and smooth.

The leg which is moving, the 'working' leg, is now

battements frappés

grand battements

grand battement *forming an* arabesque

moving freely and will work harder from now on. In the *ronds de jambes en l'air* the leg from the knee down will make a circle in the air. The working leg is raised so that the knee is almost at right angles to the body. The down-pointing foot then makes an oval in the air. This exercise also features in centre work and can often be seen in Danish ballets such as *La Sylphide*.

The class slowly progresses with *developpés* which, as the name hints, involve the slow unfolding of the leg to the front, back or side, with a well pointed foot, into an *arabesque*. Balance becomes more difficult, but the barre should be used as little as possible, as this step will have to be done totally unsupported in the centre.

Class now moves on to the *petits battements*, little beating steps which are there to prepare for the centre once more, particularly for steps such as the *entrechat*. The working leg is moving briskly from the knee down with the thigh held steady. The *grands battements* progress from these: big beating steps in which the whole leg swings from the hip. Usually the up-swing is sharp, with the down-swing slower and more controlled.

The barre is now coming to a close and should end with some personal stretching exercises to suit the dancer's own body. But even while doing these the basic rules of posture should be remembered; the *ports de bras*, the way the head and hips are held.

The dancer's body is now ready for exercises in the centre of the studio, called (surprise, surprise) centre work.

This starts with the *adage*, the slow section, which teaches balance and coordination. Now that the barre is not being used, proper *ports de bras*, with both arms, can be done. Exercises will also use a bigger number of positions of the body. Up to now the exercises have been

attitude   arabesque

done either to the side or the front. Positions such as *croisé, effacé* and *écarté* will now be introduced, each placing the body at a different angle in relation to the audience.

Centre work can vary from teacher to teacher much more than barre work, but the starting poses will all be concerned with balance. These include the *attitude*, which was copied by the great teacher Blasis at the beginning of the nineteenth century from the statue of Mercury by Giovanni da Bologna. It is a simple pose which consists of standing on one leg with the working leg raised behind the body and bent at the knee. The arm on the same side of the body as the raised leg would be in fifth with the other stretched out in second. This is the pose you would see performed on pointe when Aurora performs the balances of the Rose Adage in *The Sleeping Beauty*.

Other balancing poses include the various arabesques.

They are made by standing on one leg with the working leg raised, fully stretched, as high as possible behind you. The body should tilt naturally, making a line right through the body from outstretched toe to finger tip. The only exception is in an *arabesque penchée*, when the dancer may allow the body to tilt more to let the leg fly much higher. This is the step which is performed by the thirty-two ballerinas who fill the stage at the beginning of the 'Kingdom of the Shades' act in *La Bayadère*.

Pirouettes are the most difficult steps to describe in words. They are the many types of turning steps, and they are named after the positions in which they are performed: turns in *arabesque*, *attitude* or second position. Later in the class *fouettés*, fast, whipping turns, will be practised.

Small jumps, the *petit allegro*, will warm the dancer up for the bigger jumps later. *Changements* are the first stage towards *entrechats*, jumping up and down and changing the position of the feet.

Variations on *changements* for girls will include the *pas de chat*, literally jumping to the side, like a cat on hot bricks, with the leading leg bending on the way up and the following leg doing the same on the way down. This step appears, not surprisingly, in the variation for the White Cat in *The Sleeping Beauty*. This is a travelling jump, as are those the boys will perform, such as the *temps de poisson*, which looks like a fish jumping up out of the water and arching its spine.

Class moves on to the 'beating' steps in the centre, *batterie*. The main steps are the *entrechat*, in which the dancer jumps straight into the air and crosses the feet. They are named according to the number of changes of position of the feet, not the number of times the feet cross; *entrechat quatre*, *cinq*, *six* etc., right up to *entrechat*

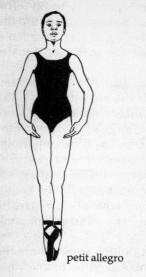

petit allegro

temps de poisson

Double work.

107

dix, which takes a slow-motion replay to identify. The simplest entrechat, *entrechat deux*, a simple jump into the air with only one change or crossing of feet, is called a *royal*. Odd numbered entrechat are explained by the dancer landing on one foot only.

The class speeds up with the *jetés*, the big, exciting jumps, cutting cleanly through the air with *ballon*, the bouncing quality every good dancer should have. More exciting turns follow, *fouettés* for the girls, *tours en l'air* for the boys. This is the basic jump in any boys' repertoire and double turns are regularly expected. At the end of the class the boys may try some more difficult steps while the girls put their shoes on for exercises *en pointe*. Young dancers must follow their teachers' advice before starting these, as doing them too young can damage not completely formed feet.

The class may also end with double work where the boy will learn how to present his ballerina, to make her feel quite secure and to give her the confidence to relax and concentrate on her own performance. The perfect partner presents his ballerina with loving care, his movements matching those of the ballerina to make a picture of harmony.

Class ends with a *révérence*, a bow. And there is usually applause for the teacher.

▓ MODERN-DANCE CLASS

Students are able to start modern-dance classes much later than classical classes. In fact, for girls in particular, it would be impossible to have a career in classical ballet unless they started early enough. An athletic boy with a suitable physique could start later; some have actually started as late as fifteen or sixteen and gone on to successful careers.

It is around this age that students start taking modern classes, often having already had a good basic training in classical dance. Indeed, some modern dance companies such as Nederlands Dans Theater mostly have classical classes, with only a few modern ones. It is also a good basis for other forms of theatre dancing, such as jazz and tap.

There are as many different systems of teaching modern dance as there are teachers. It is much more personal than classical ballet, often depending on the individual style of the teacher and how they want to express themselves on stage.

The most widespread system is based on the teachings of Martha Graham. Even if the class is not exactly as she would teach her own company, many other companies base their teaching on hers, with small changes.

Many of the most important modern choreographers, such as Merce Cunningham and Paul Taylor, have worked with her. They in turn have passed on the teaching, with their own ideas, to younger dancers and choreographers. Cunningham for instance uses the weight of the head to make balances and unbalances in class, as well as using leg movements which have more in common with classical dance.

Although the modern class works from simple warming and loosening exercises to big jumps, just like a classical class, it does not have so many individually named steps or positions.

To give you some idea of what may happen, here is the outline of a typical Graham class. Graham believes that the way the body moves should be based on the way it is made, and that it should not be worked into unnatural positions as in the classical ballet. She also thinks that dancers should follow the force of gravity, which pulls the body towards the ground. They should not fight against it and want to be light and airborne, as in classical ballet.

A Graham class is divided into three main sections: exercises with the dancer on the floor, followed by exercises standing, then exercises to help jumps and for 'falls'. These are an important part of Graham choreography.

Roughly the first half hour of a Graham class is on the floor. The floor takes the place of the classical barre, giving the dancer support and balance. In this position there are exercises to stretch the legs and to flex the foot at right angles. It is also when you come across another important Graham idea: that of contraction and release, based on breathing. Breathing in is release, breathing out is contraction. When you breathe out your pelvis curves slightly under, making the back and shoulders go rounded. When the lungs fill with air the back straightens and the shoulders settle. The same movements are repeated every day for basic teaching. Typical poses would involve sitting cross-legged, sitting with legs wide apart, or sitting on the hips with one knee bent back.

The middle half hour of class involves exercises for feet, legs and hips and uses a special form of the classical *plié* in which there is a slight turn-out, as in ballet. Many exercises would be recognizable to a classical student, except that the feet are parallel and not turned out or pointed. When beats are performed they are done with the legs still parallel.

The last half hour of the class involves modern versions of jumps and concentrates on different forms of 'fall and recovery'. A Graham-trained dancer must know how to fall to the ground in a number of ways. A knee-bend and falling backwards would be a typical example.

The class will end with various steps put together into combinations of walking steps, prancing steps, jumps and falls, working towards the way they will appear on the stage.

■ JAZZ AND TAP CLASSES

A jazz class is more like a rehearsal than a class in which individual steps are learned and practised. There will be a long warming-up period, with exercises to get the body supple and ready for work. They will start with the dancers on the floor and include exercises like the modern 'contractions' to loosen the spine. The exact exercises will depend almost entirely on the teacher's style and the reason for which the class is being given. This will mean that after the warming-up exercises the teacher will set a routine to be learned and repeated. There is no rule about the structure of the class, other than the rules your particular teacher may make up.

A well-trained classical dancer may at first feel a little stiff and formal, but with a good knowledge of basic ballet steps you will soon have the confidence to relax and enjoy a jazz class.

Tap classes are more formal. In junior classes you will learn the basic steps and possibly take the examinations of one of the stage-dance associations. But after this, classes for an experienced or professional tap-dancer will become more like a rehearsal for a performance than a class in itself.

The basic rules of practice are those for any class. Girls should have their hair up and out of the way, you should have good poise and, most important in tap-dancing, you should avoid the natural temptation to look at your feet. Except in a mirror, that is.

Just as pointe shoes are important for girls in classical ballet, so tap shoes should be of good quality and flexible. The best are lace-up shoes with a toe-tap added. Girls sometimes like a shoe with a bar over the instep, known as American bow-tie. Sometimes heel-taps are added, when you have worked through the early stages of training. Shoes should be well-tried for flexibility on your feet before you buy. Bending them by hand can be very misleading.

Before you start tapping with your feet it is important to try out beating time by clapping your hands, trying to repeat different and ever more complicated rhythms. You will need to feel the time, which is the beat of the music, the tempo, which is the speed at which it is played and the rhythm or musical pattern.

Once again you will warm up before setting out on the steps. For tap special attention is paid to the ankles, as it is from here that most of the action will come. Holding a support (it need not be a barre) lift your foot (wearing your tap shoes) and point it toe down, then up like a hinge, for the number of times your teacher sets. Repeat with the other foot. Still supported you should then circle the foot from the ankle, with the toe pointing up. Again repeat this according to your teacher's instructions.

Bouncing up and down follows, which in classical terms means going up to half point and back down again, but with your arms swinging up and down freely to give a bouncing feel. After this you can jump and clap, which not only warms you, but also starts moving towards learning the coordination of actions. As you bounce up, this time leaving the floor, you clap. Your teacher will then suggest variations, mixing the bounces and the claps to different rhythms. These jumps and claps can also be done sideways.

Walking to music is also important in a tap class, to develop timing. For young beginners, marching and skipping is an enjoyable exercise. Walking then develops into gallops, which do not mean wildly running round like a horse. Instead these are sideways travelling steps which, when you are more advanced, can include clicking your heels when they meet in the air. You see this step in national dances such as the mazurka.

You are now working towards the first real tap steps, for which you should stand on the ball of one foot, which, as in ballet, is called the supporting foot. Extend the working foot forward, raised a little from the ground. You then tap the ground sharply with the ball of your working foot, turning your toe up so that your ankle joint is producing the upward movement.

Now that you are on the way to tapping, you will following your teacher's instructions through exercises in which you will learn to do single taps forward and backward, which will become a shuffle when you do them quickly together. You will also learn how to change feet during a sequence, transferring weight from one foot to another. And then there are stamps, putting your flat foot down very firmly, ball, heel and toe taps and steps with names such as cramp rolls, stomps, brushes, scuffs, flaps and time steps. As with ballet, the names of the steps give you some idea of the sort of movements they are.

Unlike classical ballet, jazz and tap-dance can be done for enjoyment only. Even modern dance can be started late and has proved very popular with students up to university level, when it would be impossible to take up ballet.

YOU PUT YOUR RIGHT FOOT IN
Making a Dance

Making dances is difficult to explain in detail, as so much of the work depends upon the personality of the people involved: those thinking up the steps and the dancers trying to do them. It is not just a question of choosing steps from those done in class and putting one after another. Each choreographer has to change the classroom steps in small ways to create new images. It is more like a painter applying paint to a canvas, choosing different shades of the same colour or using different brush strokes to create different needs. In ballet it is the choreographer who is the painter, the dancers are his colours and the studio and the stage are his canvases.

■ THE CHOREOGRAPHER

There are as many ways of making ballets as there are choreographers. They are the people who mastermind the whole production. They first choose the music and subject, then the dancers and then the designer.

When the great court ballets were created in the late sixteenth century, the ballet masters had to be much more like army generals, organizing their forces across great courtyards, giving complicated patterns for the horses to follow, arranging for the entries of the acrobats or mime artists, not to mention the huge decorated carriages which carried in the food. As well as this they had to arrange the courtiers, in the formal dances like the minuet or the galliard.

These ballet masters used violins to give the rhythms of the dance up to the nineteenth century, when the piano slowly came into use. And now the piano in turn is occasionally replaced by the cassette-player.

During the Romantic age and the great age of the classical ballet in Russia nearly all the music which the choreographers used was written specially for the ballet. Usually it was written to order, which explains why so much of it is rather simple and uncomplicated.

When *Giselle* was being choreographed by Jean Coralli and Jules Perrot, the music was written, in only a week, by Adolph Adam, and then extra pieces, such as the peasant *pas de deux*, were added by another composer. Few composers would allow this to happen today.

When Marius Petipa created the great classical ballets, *Swan Lake* and *The Sleeping Beauty*, he asked Tchaikovsky to write the music. He gave him very detailed notes about what he wanted and then left Tchaikovsky to produce music of exactly the right length and tempo. It is amazing that under these circumstances the music he wrote is so great, some of the most beautiful in ballet. Petipa's notes still exist and show the exact details he gave Tchaikovsky. In the second act of *The Sleeping Beauty*, when Aurora is tricked into handling the spindle on which she will prick her finger, Petipa told the story to Tchaikovsky with exact instructions about what he wanted. He wrote:

Aurora notices an old woman who beats out 2/4 time with the spindle in her hand. As this changes to a 3/4 tempo, very gay, Aurora takes the spindle which she waves about. She shows everyone how delighted she is – 24 bars of a waltz. But suddenly she pricks her fingers and blood flows – eight bars of 4/4 tempo. Full of terror as though she had been bitten by a tarantula spider. She turns and falls – all this should take twenty-four to thirty-two bars. She cries to her mother and father – a few bars tremolo. The old woman reveals herself as the wicked fairy Carabosse – the orchestra play a great scale. As Carabosse leaves the four princes run away in terror – then magical, tender music which must last until the end of the act while the Lilac Fairy promises that Aurora will not die, but sleep for a hundred years. Aurora and the court slowly fall to sleep and a forest grows around them.

Few modern composers would work this way and, in any case, not much music is specially written for ballet now.

If a choreographer is making a full-evening story ballet he will possibly work with a writer and construct the story. He will then find existing music to suit the mood or the action and have it arranged as he wants.

The way choreographers work with dancers is different from person to person. Someone like Kenneth MacMillan is influenced by the personality of his dancers. Jiri Kylián of Nederlans Dans Theater is influenced by the technical ability of his dancers. George Balanchine wanted his dancers to do nothing except the steps as he taught them; he did not want them to introduce any of their own personality into his choreography.

In dance pieces without a story, which are called abstract dances, the dancers can make a real contribution, suggesting steps or ways to make the choreographers ideas work more smoothly. Often in rehearsal a dancer has tried out a step or even fallen over and the choreographer has said, 'Keep that step in.' This happened in Balanchine's *Serenade*, which he created for his first students at the School of American Ballet in 1934. One girl fell over, another arrived late, and both incidents were kept in the ballet.

Often a choreographer will arrange the dancers into some complicated pose and ask them to work out a way to get out of it smoothly.

Choreography for musicals has changed over the years as much as that for the ballet. In the great days of the Broadway musical in the 1930s the dances were for entertainment only and did not bother with characters or emotions. Usually there were lots of chorus girls and boys doing very simple steps. As long as they all did them together it looked spectacular. Even when great ballet choreographers such as George Balanchine worked in Broadway shows such as *On Your Toes*, the effect looked more or less the same.

Slowly this began to change and Agnes de Mille created the first serious dance number in the musical *Oklahoma!* This dance sequence was not just for entertainment. It showed Laurie's problems and explained the story in a more dramatic way than would have been possible in song.

Jerome Robbins used his ballet *Fancy Free* as the basis for both a musical and a film, *On The Town*. This was the story of three American sailors having a day off in New York. A few years later he created *West Side Story*; the story of Romeo and Juliet moved to the west side of New York. He made real characters through the dancing: the rival gangs, the Sharks and Jets and the two lovers, Maria and Tony.

The choreographer Michael Bennett showed the struggles of show dancers in the brilliant musical *A*

Chorus Line, with each dance reflecting the different personality and problems of the dancers. It also showed the hard work the dancer has to do to create the magical illusion on the stage.

■ THE BALLET MASTER

The title ballet master has changed over the years. Originally it referred to the person in charge of the ballet, creating the steps. Now it refers to the person who is in day-to-day charge of the dancers, giving the daily class and organizing and supervising rehearsals. Most big companies have more than one ballet master to do the many different jobs which are their responsibility. Even small companies will have guest ballet masters to give the dancers some variety in the teaching.

One ballet master will be more concerned with teaching, another with rehearsing certain ballets. In the Royal Ballet, for example, one will look after Frederick Ashton's ballets, while another will look after Kenneth MacMillan's. And yet another will only be concerned with teaching. Those who look after rehearsals can also be called *répétiteurs*, which is French for coaches or tutors.

The job of the ballet master is a difficult one, as they have to deal with the dancers every day, often taking rehearsals where a few simple steps may have to be repeated over and over again until they are perfect. This can lead to bad moods, arguments and tiredness which the ballet master has to smooth over. They will also watch all the performances and take notes of things which go wrong, steps, acting or costume. To give small corrections they will go backstage as soon as the curtain falls and speak to each dancer individually. If things have been particularly bad they may have to call the whole company to rehearse a complete scene, or the whole ballet, the next day.

In the world of the musical the ballet master is called the dance captain, usually someone who is also a member of the cast. In recent years, as the amount and complexity of dancing in shows such as *Cats* has increased, an additional dance captain has been appointed to give classes and take rehearsals when the choreographer is not available. It will be up to the dance captain to rehearse new members of the cast so that they will be ready for the busy choreographer to polish the performances before the dancers appear on the stage.

Ballet masters, like dancers, have brilliant memories for steps and can remember dozens of ballets. But nowadays they have several means of helping their memories. The oldest system is notation: the system of writing ballets down.

■ THE NOTATOR

Different ways of writing ballets down have existed since ballet started in the fifteenth century. These early forms of notation were special to each ballet master and few other people could understand them.

A book describing how dances should be performed was published as early as 1588 by Thoinot Arbeau, but the first notation system for general use was published in Paris in 1700 by Raoul Feuillet. It was based on material supplied by Beauchamp, the ballet master at the Académie Royale de la Danse. It became known outside France and was translated into English only six years later, which was very fast for the time. The system showed the track on the floor which the dancers followed, with signs on music lines to show turns and beats. This system was used until the French Revolution, when it fell out of use: many of the aristocracy (who did most of the dancing) had been killed.

There was no new system to replace it for many years, though different ballet masters used stick-figure systems to remind them of steps. At the end of the nineteenth century in St Petersburg the Russian dancer Vladimir Stepanov devised another system which used lines, like music, but only three of them, onto which details of the movements were put. This system became very important for Britain as it was from his notes of the classical ballets of Petipa that Nikolai Sergeyev was able to put on *The Sleeping Beauty*, first for Serge Diaghilev in 1921, and later for Ninette de Valois and the young Royal Ballet.

In 1928, Rudolf Laban, an important person in modern dance, published his own system which, for the first time, could show by the length of the symbol how long certain steps should take. This system is still widely used, but not as widely as the system known as 'choreology'. It is now so widespread that the word is often used to mean all methods of writing dance steps down. In fact it was developed by Rudolf and Joan Benesh (he was an artist and she was a dancer with the Royal Ballet) and was known as Benesh Notation for many years.

It started as a sort of shorthand reminder of ballet, but after the Royal Ballet started using it, it soon spread around the world. It uses simplified stick figures with other symbols on music paper, the writer showing the dance position and the movements on the music lines, with special signs being added to show placing and timing. Choreology is the most flexible system and is used in the fields of modern dance, the musical and even in some

Examples of Benesh Notation, commonly known as choreology, and the movements they describe.

sports such as ice-skating and synchronized swimming.

Most classical companies now have notators to write down ballets as they are created. These records are used for rehearsals when there is doubt about how a step should be performed or even what the steps should be. Some choreographers have used film to record ballets, but these are not so good for rehearsals. Once a company learned a ballet by Léonide Massine backwards, as the film had not been rewound correctly.

The invention of video has been a great help to dancers and ballet masters, as it is much more convenient than film. Companies such as Nederlands Dans Theater have used video for many years, but it is best for an individual dancer to learn the steps alone before joining the main rehearsals. For a whole company to learn from videos would be awkward, as the dancers have to look over their shoulders to get the correct positions! In fact what really happens is that the dancers watch the video, memorizing the steps, and then perform without looking at the screen.

Although all these systems are now widely used, the best way of handing down a ballet from generation to generation is for older dancers to teach younger dancers. All the systems you have read about can explain the steps correctly, and some can show the correct speed they should be done. But what they cannot do is hand down the correct style with which the steps should be danced. It is much better for a great ballerina such as Alicia Markova to explain to a young dancer how a ballet should be done. If she is teaching *Les Sylphides*, she can explain exactly what its choreographer, Mikhail Fokine, intended as she worked with him the last time he put on his ballet, in the 1940s. This way of working gives a young dancer a direct link with a ballet's creator or through him to the Imperial Ballet of Russia almost a century ago.

■ THE MUSICIANS

Although there have been ballets and modern dances performed without music (Jerome Robbin's *Moves* is the most famous), music is essential for the dance, from Tchaikovsky to jazz. Even those ballets which have been danced without it have depended on the dancers counting to rhythms learned in the studio.

The first music a young dancer will come across is in class. Often this is just special music written specifically for classes, sometimes boring and uninspiring. There are now many composers writing much more interesting music for classes (these are usually advertised in magazines such as the *Dancing Times*) and at professional level pianists use a wide range of tunes to make the class more enjoyable.

Dancing on stage can often bring problems with musicians unless there is a conductor who particularly likes ballet. He or she has to keep watch on the stage as well as on the musicians to make sure that everyone keeps together. Often it is impossible for a dancer to perform steps at exactly the speed a composer has written the music and the conductor has to be prepared to adjust the tempo to suit the dancer. Some do not like to do this and insist on their own tempo. The result is that dancers can be left looking as though they have done something wrong, even though it may be physically impossible to pirouette or jump at the speed the conductor is taking the music. The musicians' motto is: the dancer is always wrong.

■ THE DESIGNER

Design plays an important part in all ballets. For the dancer the costume designs are the most important, as it is essential that they can move freely, be able to jump and turn, while still dressed as the designer wishes. Some designers working in the dance world for the first time might want tight trousers or dresses with lots of hanging ribbons or decorations, not realizing at first that they will risk strangling the ballerina, or make it impossible to lift legs. Many times an unfortunate prince has nearly been blinded by a flying piece of heavy costume-jewellery not properly attached to a tutu. Dancers have to have the ability to look good in clothes which may be completely unsuited to their shapes or their looks. This requires great confidence, which can only come from careful training and a belief in the part being played.

■ WHO'S WHO IN DANCE

There are a few people who are particularly important in the dance world. They appear throughout the story of dance in this book. Here are a few more details about them.

■ **SIR FREDERICK ASHTON** was born in Ecuador, South America, in 1904. He died in 1988. When he was thirteen he saw Anna Pavlova dance in Peru and decided that he wanted to become a ballet dancer. He went to London, where he studied with Marie Rambert who encouraged his first attempt at choreography, a short ballet called *A Tragedy of Fashion*. He became Britain's greatest choreographer. Ballets you can still enjoy include *Symphonic Variations*, *A Wedding Bouquet*, *La Fille Mal Gardée*, *A Month in the Country* and many other works which are danced all around the world. In 1980 he created the ballet *Rhapsody* for Queen Elizabeth the Queen Mother's eightieth birthday and in 1986 he made a short ballet for the Queen's sixtieth birthday. In 1985 his version of *Romeo and Juliet* was revived by Peter Schaufuss for London Festival Ballet. The role of Juliet had originally been created for Schaufuss's mother, the Danish ballerina Mona Vangsaae, and the Royal Danish Ballet in 1955.

■ **FRED ASTAIRE** was already dancing on stage with his sister Adele when he was seven. He was born in 1899, and by the time he was twenty he and Adele were musical-comedy stars in both New York and London. When he was screen-tested for Hollywood movies, they said that he couldn't sing, couldn't act, but could dance a little! He made his first film with Joan Crawford in 1933 and in the same year danced with Ginger Rogers in the film *Flying Down to Rio*. The couple went on to star in several of the best musicals made in Hollywood in the 1930s. He rehearsed his dance routines by himself for weeks before teaching them to Ginger Rogers and then they were filmed, often in one take. Films, such as *Top Hat* are shown on television, so we can still enjoy his extremely elegant and relaxed manner, as well as his brilliant tap-dancing.

■ **GEORGE BALANCHINE** was born in Russia in 1904 and studied dance and music at the Imperial Ballet School in Petrograd (as St Petersburg had been re-named after the Russian Revolution in 1917, before it was changed once more, to Leningrad). He graduated into the state ballet company in 1921. In 1924 he left Russia with a group of dancer friends and eventually joined the Diaghilev Ballet in France as ballet master and dancer. It was there that he started choreographing. In 1928 he created *Apollo* to music by Stravinsky, who became his favourite composer. After Diaghilev's death in 1929 he worked in London, Copenhagen and Monte Carlo before accepting an invitation from Lincoln Kirstein to start a school and a company in the United States. The school became the School of American Ballet (SAB) and over the years it has produced many great dancers. In 1946 he started Ballet Society, which later became the world-famous New York City Ballet. George Balanchine, always known as 'Mr B.', is without doubt one of the greatest choreographers of the twentieth century. His ballets are danced by most of the world's major companies, but none do them better than the dancers of New York City Ballet. He died in 1983.

■ MIKHAIL BARYSHNIKOV was born in Latvia in 1948, studied in Leningrad and became a soloist with the Kirov Ballet there in 1967. In the summer of 1974, while he was touring Canada with a group of dancers from the Bolshoi Ballet, he decided to stay in the West. He joined American Ballet Theater and has become one of the biggest ballet stars in the world. Audiences cheer his astonishing technique. He has danced all the major classical roles and appeared in modern ballets with equal success. He has starred in three films: *The Turning Point*, *White Nights* and *Dancers*, as well as several television 'specials'. These have made him one of the few male ballet dancers whose name is as familiar to those who know little about ballet as it is to ballet lovers.

Mikhail Baryshnikov.

■ **MAURICE BÉJART** was born in 1927 and is one of the most popular choreographers in Europe. After dancing with several companies and forming his own in 1953, he founded the Ballet du XXième Siècle (Ballet of the Twentieth Century) based in Brussels until 1987, when it moved to Lausanne, Switzerland. It has appeared in theatres, circuses, universities and even in temples. Béjart's ballets are often more popular with general theatre audiences than with people who like pure classical ballet.

■ **DAVID BINTLEY** was born in Sheffield, Britain, in 1957 and was a pupil at the Royal Ballet School in London. When he graduated he joined Sadler's Wells Royal Ballet where he established himself as an excellent character dancer, giving one of the greatest performances in the tragic story of *Petrushka*. He started to create his own ballets early on, and has become one of the best young choreographers of pure dance works as well as dramatic ballets such as *The Snow Queen* (based on the Hans Christian Andersen story).

■ **AUGUST BOURNONVILLE** was born in Copenhagen in 1805 and entered the Royal Danish Ballet School as a child. He later studied in Paris with Auguste Vestris before returning to Copenhagen in 1828 as soloist, teacher, ballet master and choreographer with the Royal Danish Ballet. His version of *La Sylphide* was first staged in Copenhagen in 1836 and has been danced there ever since. He went on to create more than fifty ballets and *divertissements* such as *Napoli*, *The Kermesse in Bruges*, *A Folk Tale*, *Flower Festival at Genzano* and *Far from Denmark*. Today Bournonville's ballets are danced all over the world, but rarely better than by the Danes who are trained in the unique Bournonville style of dancing as soon as they first enter the Royal Danish Ballet School.

JEAN COCTEAU was neither a dancer nor a choreographer, but as an artist, poet, writer and film director he had a great influence on the ballet. When he first met Diaghilev, the Russian said, 'Astonish me!' Cocteau did just that with his ideas for unusual and controversial ballets such as *Parade* (1917) in which the dancers wore huge puppet costumes designed by Picasso, and one dance is performed to the 'music' of a typewriter.

JOHN CRANKO came to London from South Africa to study at the Sadler's Wells Ballet School and appeared as a dancer with the company in 1947. Four years later his ballet *Pineapple Poll* was a great success. He followed this with more ballets, such as *The Lady and the Fool*. He also produced a revue called *Cranks*, which used many clever and inventive dance ideas and which influenced other people in the theatre. In 1961 he was invited to direct the Stuttgart Ballet in Germany. He turned it into one of Europe's best companies and created many ballets for it, including *Romeo and Juliet*, *Onegin* and *Taming of the Shrew*, all of which are still danced by many other ballet companies. His great ballerina was Marcia Haydée, who now directs the company he put on the international dance map.

MERCE CUNNINGHAM is one of the most important innovators in modern dance. He joined the Martha Graham Company in 1939 and stayed with her until 1945, creating leading roles in ballets such as *Appalachian Spring*. When he left Graham he gave solo concerts all over the United States before founding his own company in 1952. It has become one of the most influential modern dance companies in the world.

■ **AGNES DE MILLE** was a niece of the famous film director Cecil B. de Mille. She was born in 1909 and after graduating from the University of Southern California she came to London to study dance with Marie Rambert. When she returned to the United States in 1940 she joined American Ballet Theater. She had her first great success as a choreographer in 1942 with *Rodeo*, and as well as creating the choreography in such Broadway successes as *Oklahoma!*, *Brigadoon* and *Paint Your Wagon*, she went on to make other ballets including *Fall River Legend*, about Lizzie Borden (who killed her parents with an axe).

■ **NINETTE DE VALOIS**, who was born in 1898, first danced on stage in a pantomime at the Lyceum Theatre in London when she was a child. She danced with Diaghilev's Ballets Russes before founding the Academy of Choreographic Art in London in 1926. An able choreographer, she created dramatic ballets such as *The Rake's Progress* and *Checkmate*, but she is more important as a brilliant organizer and the founder of the Vic-Wells Ballet which, after several changes of name, became Britain's Royal Ballet in 1956. She officially retired in 1971, but continues to be very influential in the dance world. She was responsible for the founding of the National Ballet of Turkey and was important in the early planning of the National Ballets of Canada, Australia and Iran. She is known to all dancers and ballet lovers as 'Madame'.

■ **SERGE DIAGHILEV**, born in Russia in 1872, was sent to St Petersburg (now Leningrad) to study law, but his real love was the arts. He became the centre of a group of artistic friends who were passionately interested in ballet. In 1909 he took a group of Russian dancers and opera singers to Paris, where they were a sensation. His Ballets Russes toured all over Europe with dancers such as Pavlova, Karsavina, Massine and Nijinsky. His choreographers included Fokine, Nijinska (Nijinsky's sister) and the young Balanchine. His company commissioned scores from Stravinsky, Poulenc, Satie, Prokofiev and other leading composers of the day. Great painters such as Picasso and Rouault painted scenery for him. Ballets staged by the Ballets Russes include *The Firebird*, *Le Sacre du Printemps*, *L'Après-midi d'un Faune*, *Petrushka*, *Les Noces* and *Apollo*. He died in Venice in 1929, probably the most important figure in ballet in the twentieth century.

■ **ANTHONY DOWELL** was born in London in 1943. His first dancing teacher was film-star Susan Hampshire's mother. He went to the Royal Ballet School and joined the Royal Ballet in 1961. He was soon recognized as the finest male classical dancer in the Royal Ballet and has danced all the major roles with enormous success. His partnership with Antoinette Sibley is one of the most famous in ballet history. Frederick Ashton choreographed the roles of Oberon and Titania for them in *The Dream*, and Kenneth MacMillan created the roles of Des Grieux and Manon Lescaut for them in *Manon*. In 1986 Dowell was appointed Artistic Director of the Royal Ballet.

■ **ISADORA DUNCAN**, who was born in San Francisco in 1878, was one of the founders of modern dance. When she danced she wore flowing dresses which often showed more of her body than audiences of the day were used to. Some were shocked, but many others were impressed by her dramatic dancing. Her tragic life included the death of her children by drowning and she died in 1927 when her long scarf caught in the axle of her car and she was strangled. Although most of the dances she performed have long been forgotten, she remains one of the most influential figures in the history of dance.

■ **MIKHAIL FOKINE** was the choreographer who helped to bring ballet into the twentieth century. While he was still a dancer with the Imperial Ballet in St Petersburg he started to teach and choreograph in a way which was very different to Marius Petipa's style. One of his earliest dances was *The Dying Swan* (for Anna Pavlova) in 1907, and for the early seasons of the Ballets Russes in Paris in 1909 and 1910 he made *Les Sylphides*, *Le Spectre de la Rose*, *Sheherazade*, *The Firebird*, *Petrushka* and *Daphnis and Chloe*. Towards the end of his life he worked in America with the different Ballets Russes companies and American Ballet Theater, for whom he made his last ballet. He died in 1942.

■ **MARGOT FONTEYN** was born in 1919 and spent part of her childhood in China, where she started to go to ballet classes and in Shanghai met the great teacher Vera Volkova. In 1934 she joined the Vic-Wells Ballet. Within a few years she had danced most of the major classic roles. Sir Frederick Ashton created some of his best ballets for her, including *Ondine*. When she turned forty everyone thought that she would soon retire, but in 1963 she met the young Rudolf Nureyev. They became the greatest partnership in ballet and Frederick Ashton made *Marguerite and Armand* for them. She continued to be the prima ballerina assoluta of the Royal Ballet, performing up to the age of sixty. She now spends much of her time in her husband's home country, Panama, but returns to Britain to carry out her duties as President of the Royal Academy of Dancing.

Margot Fonteyn rehearsing The Sleeping Beauty *for a BBC Television production in 1959.*

■ **MARTHA GRAHAM** who was born in 1894 is one of the founders of modern dance. When she started her first modern-dance company in the 1920s, audiences did not like her choreography. But she persisted and became the most important figure in the development of modern dance in America. She danced with her company until she was almost eighty, in ballets such as *Night Journey* and *Clytemnestra*, and she is still creating dances, though now well into her nineties. In 1976 she was awarded America's highest civilian award, the Medal of Freedom.

■ **ROBERT HELPMANN**, an Australian dancer born in 1909, made his name with the Vic-Wells Ballet in the 1930s, dancing with Alicia Markova and Margot Fonteyn. He was equally at home in classic roles like Albrecht and comic ones such as the Ugly Sister in Sir Frederick Ashton's *Cinderella*. He appeared in the films *The Red Shoes* and *Tales of Hoffmann* and was an important figure in establishing male dancing in Britain. He returned to Australia in the 1960s to create ballets for the young Australian Ballet of which he was Director from 1965 to 1976. He died in 1988.

■ **TAMARA KARSAVINA**, born 1885, trained at the Imperial Ballet School in St Petersburg and became a soloist with the company in 1902. Her biography *Theatre Street* charmingly describes life at the school. By 1909 she was dancing ballerina roles and with Fokine and Nijinsky took part in the early Diaghilev seasons in Paris, creating such roles as the Doll in *Petrushka*. She escaped from Russia during the Revolution of 1917 and eventually settled in London and made an important contribution to British ballet, coaching Margot Fonteyn and other ballerinas in the roles that she had danced until her death at the age of ninety-three in 1978. She also helped Sir Frederick Ashton with his production of *La Fille Mal Gardée*, a ballet she had danced in St Petersburg more than fifty years before.

GELSEY KIRKLAND was born in Pennsylvania in 1953 and studied at the School of American Ballet where Balanchine spotted her great talent. She danced many important roles for New York City Ballet before joining American Ballet Theater, where she was hailed as one of the finest classical ballerinas of her generation. In London she has been acclaimed for her superb interpretation of Juliet when she performed with the Royal Ballet at Covent Garden. Her life story, *Dancing on my Grave*, is a terrible tale of how hard a dancer's life can be.

JIRI KYLIÁN is the Czech-born (1947) Artistic Director of Nederlands Dans Theater. He was a pupil at the Royal Ballet School in London and in 1968 joined Stuttgart Ballet, where he began to choreograph. He has developed a personal, athletic style which can be seen in *Symphony of Psalms*, *Soldier's Mass* and the other ballets he has created since moving to Holland in 1976.

LEONID LAVROSKY studied at the former Imperial Ballet School in Leningrad, joined the company there as a dancer in 1922, and started to teach and choreograph early in his career. In 1935, when he was only thirty, he became director of the Maly Theatre in Leningrad, and three years later was appointed Director of the Kirov Ballet. He created *Romeo and Juliet* in 1940: the first of the big Russian ballets, it would become typical of the Bolshoi Ballet in particular. His Juliet was Galina

Ulanova. He was twice Director of the Bolshoi and in 1964 was appointed Director of the Bolshoi School. His son Mikhail became one of the greatest male dancers in the Soviet Union.

■ **SERGE LIFAR** was only eighteen when he left Russia to join Diaghilev's company in 1923. Lifar was poorly trained so Diaghilev made him study with the company teacher, Enrico Cecchetti, and the young Russian became an outstandingly handsome dancer. He created roles in two of the great ballets Balanchine made for the company – *The Prodigal Son* and *Apollo*. In 1929 he went to dance at the Paris Opéra and remained there, with a few breaks, until 1957 as dancer and, later, ballet master and choreographer. He was responsible for re-establishing ballet in Paris, encouraging young ballerinas in the 1930s, including Yvette Chauviré and Nina Vyroubova.

Kenneth MacMillan.

■ **KENNETH MACMILLAN** was born in 1929 and started his ballet career as a dancer with Sadler's Wells Theatre Ballet. He had his first success as a choreographer in 1955 with *Danses Concertantes*. He went on to produce many superb ballets for the Royal Ballet and for other companies. They include: *The Invitation*, *Romeo and Juliet*, *Manon*, *Anastasia* and *Elite Syncopations*, many of which are regularly danced by companies all around the world. He left London for New York in 1985 to work with American Ballet Theater.

■ **NATALIA MAKAROVA** was born in 1940 and trained at the famous Vaganova School (named after the great Russian ballerina) in L'eningrad. She danced with the Kirov Ballet before settling in the West in 1970 and joining American Ballet Theater. She made her debut in *Giselle*, which is one of her most famous roles. She quickly became one of the best-known ballerinas in the world, dancing roles such as Juliet, Roland Petit's *Carmen*, Odette-Odile in *Swan Lake* and Tatyana in Cranko's *Onegin*. She has also appeared with great success in the Broadway musical *On Your Toes*, in which she played a Russian ballerina, winning a Tony Award for her performance.

■ **ALICIA MARKOVA** was the first British prima ballerina. Born in London in 1910, she first appeared in pantomimes. She took classes with Serafina Astafieva, where she met the young Patrick Healy-Kay who, as Anton Dolin, would become her partner. Together they would also found London Festival Ballet. At the age of twelve Markova joined the Diaghilev company and Balanchine made *Le Rossignol* (*The Nightingale*) for her. After Diaghilev's death she came back to Britain in time for the birth of British ballet. She joined Ballet Rambert and created roles in some of the early Ashton ballets such as *Façade* before joining the Vic-Wells Ballet run by Ninette de Valois. She was the first British dancer to perform the roles of Giselle and Odette-Odile. She went to America to dance with the newly formed American Ballet Theater, returning to Britain in 1948 to dance with Dolin at Sadler's Wells Ballet. She retired as a dancer in 1962, but has taught and lectured since. She told her own story in the book *Markova Remembers*.

■ **PETER MARTINS** was trained at the Royal Danish Ballet School. He was quickly promoted to principal, but in 1969, at the age of twenty-three, went to the United States to join the New York City Ballet. He was soon recognized as the finest male dancer of the City Ballet's repertoire and Balanchine created several ballets for him. Martins has also choreographed ballets for the company and before Balanchine died he was appointed joint director of the company with Jerome Robbins.

■ **LÉONIDE MASSINE** became Diaghilev's choreographer and principal dancer after Nijinsky married and left the Ballets Russes. Diaghilev guided Massine's career and was rewarded with some excellent ballets including *La Boutique Fantasque* and *Le Tricorne* (both 1919). After Diaghilev died and his Ballets Russes came to an end, Massine became the leading choreographer (and dancer) with the Ballets Russes de Monte Carlo. He created ballets to well-known symphonies, which was a new idea in the 1930s, but as he got older he did not have the great success he had had with the ballets of his youth. These early ballets are still danced by many companies today.

■ **JOHN NEUMEIER** is an American dancer and choreographer who has made his name in Europe. He studied in Chicago and London before dancing with John Cranko's company in Stuttgart, where he began to choreograph. In 1969 he was appointed Director of Frankfurt Ballet and four years later moved to Hamburg to direct the company there.

■ **VASLAV NIJINSKY** was born in 1888 in Kiev, where his dancer parents were working, and he went to the Imperial Ballet School in St Petersburg. It was soon obvious that he had a special talent and an amazing technique, as well as unusual Oriental features. He was one of the group of dancers Diaghilev took to Paris, where he was a sensation as the Golden Slave in *Scheherazade*. Diaghilev encouraged him to choreograph and his ballets, *L'Après-midi d'un Faune* and *Le Sacre du Printemps*, caused riots in the theatre. They were the first really modern ballets of the twentieth century, with unusual steps and difficult music. Early in his life, Nijinsky showed signs of mental illness and in 1917 he became seriously ill. From then until his death in London in 1950 he spent long periods of his life in mental homes. Nijinsky's younger sister, Bronislava Nijinska, was also a talented dancer and choreographer. Her ballets *Les Biches* and *Les Noces* were great successes in London when they were revived in the mid-1960s, forty years after they were created.

■ **RUDOLF NUREYEV** was born on a train in Russia in 1938. By 1961 he was one of the leading dancers with the Kirov Ballet, but when the company was on tour in Paris, afraid that he would be sent back to the Soviet Union and not given the chance to dance leading roles,

Rudolf Nureyev.

he asked for political asylum after escaping from the Soviet guards who were about to bundle him onto a Russia-bound plane. He had a tremendous impact on audiences wherever he danced, but especially in Britain, where a whole generation of male dancers were influenced by his athleticism and his artistry. He created a memorable partnership with Dame Margot Fonteyn, who had arranged for him to dance in London shortly after he escaped to the West. He has danced in ballets by modern-dance choreographers such as Martha Graham and Glen Tetley and has put on many of his own productions, including *The Nutcracker* for the Royal Ballet and *Romeo and Juliet* for London Festival Ballet. He still dances, but spends much of his time with the Paris Opéra, where he is Artistic Director.

■ **MERLE PARK** was born in Rhodesia (now Zimbabwe) in 1937. She trained as a dancer in Surrey before joining the Sadler's Wells Ballet in 1954. She was made a

■ 140

principal five years later. She has danced all the major roles in the classical repertoire and created roles in *Shadowplay*, *Jazz Calendar* and *Mayerling*. She is now a Dame of the British Empire and Principal of the Royal Ballet School.

■ **ANNA PAVLOVA** was born in 1881 and trained at the Imperial Ballet School in St Petersburg, performing in the famous Maryinsky Theatre before she graduated. She danced in the early Diaghilev seasons, but settled in London in 1912. Pavlova created her own company and danced around the world, in grand theatres and on tiny stages alike, taking ballet to a huge audience, from Austria to Australia, Norway to New Zealand (where the Pavlova – a meringue dessert – was created in her honour). She died on tour in 1931.

■ **MARIUS PETIPA** was born in France in 1818 and died in Russia in 1910. For nearly forty years he dominated ballet in Russia, taking over from Arthur Saint-Léon as Chief Ballet Master at the Imperial Theatre in St Petersburg in 1869 after having been a principal dancer with the company for more than twenty years. Petipa was responsible for creating classical ballet as we know it today. He worked closely with Tchaikovsky to create first *The Sleeping Beauty* and then *The Nutcracker*.

■ **ROLAND PETIT** trained at the Paris Opera Ballet School in Paris and joined the company after he graduated in 1940. In 1945 he was one of the dancers who founded the Ballets des Champs-Elysées, a company which became very popular in Europe. In 1948 he founded the Ballets de Paris, for which he produced his most famous ballet, *Carmen*, with his wife Zizi Jeanmaire in the title role. In 1972 he took over the Ballet de Marseille, which he has made the second most important company in France.

■ **MARIE RAMBERT** was born in Poland in 1888. She trained in early modern dance and helped Nijinsky to choreograph *Le Sacre du Printemps*. She became interested in classical ballet mainly due to the influence of Karsavina. She came to London in 1918 and opened a school in 1920, with Frederick Ashton as one of her early pupils. The Marie Rambert Dancers became Ballet Club and later the Ballet Rambert, England's oldest ballet company. Marie Rambert had an amazing ability to recognize talented choreographers, designers and dancers before anyone else. The company is now Britain's most famous modern ballet company. The young talent that she spotted has been very influential. Apart from Ashton, others who worked with Rambert include:

Marie Rambert.

Anthony Tudor, Agnes de Mille, Alicia Markova, Robert Helpmann and Norman Morrice, who became Director of the Royal Ballet. Mim, as Dame Marie was known, worked with her company until she was ninety years old, attending every first night and keenly watching all the new, modern choreography. She died in 1982.

■■ **JEROME ROBBINS** choreographs ballets and Broadway shows with equal ability. He began his career as a dancer in Broadway musicals before joining American Ballet Theater in 1940. In 1944 he created his first ballet, *Fancy Free*, which is the only ballet to have been turned into a Broadway musical and a Hollywood movie, both called *On The Town*. His ballet *The Concert* is one of the few really funny ballets, and his *Dances at a Gathering* is one of the most beautiful works of pure dance. For Broadway he created *West Side Story* and directed *Fiddler on the Roof*. He also created the ballet *The Little House of Uncle Tom* in the film *The King and I*. He is now joint director of the New York City Ballet.

■■ **PETER SCHAUFUSS** was born in 1949 and trained at the famous Royal Danish Ballet School in Copenhagen, where both of his parents were leading dancers. Shortly after he graduated into the Royal Danish Ballet he left for the National Ballet Canada, but returned home a season later. He then joined London Festival Ballet and began to make guest appearances with other companies in Europe and America. He joined New York City Ballet for two years, but left to become one of the most acclaimed globe-trotting male dancers of his generation. He staged *La Sylphide* for London Festival Ballet in 1979 and went on to produce *Napoli* for the National Ballet of Canada. He is now Artistic Director of London Festival Ballet.

■ **MOIRA SHEARER** was Margot Fonteyn's rival for public affection when they were both ballerinas with Sadler's Wells Ballet in the 1940s and early 1950s. She danced all the classical roles and created the title role in Ashton's *Cinderella* in 1948. She will always be remembered by ballet lovers as the beautiful red-haired star of the film *The Red Shoes*, which introduced more people to dance than any ballet ever did.

■ **ANTOINETTE SIBLEY** joined the Royal Ballet School in 1949, when she was ten. She joined the company in 1956 and was made a principal dancer in 1960. Later that year she had to dance the leading role in *Swan Lake* at very short notice and had a great triumph. Since then she has created the roles of Titania in Ashton's *The Dream* and the title role in MacMillan's *Manon*. Her partnership with Anthony Dowell was one of the most important in the history of the Royal Ballet.

■ **IGOR STRAVINSKY** is the most important composer for twentieth-century ballet. Born in Russia in 1882, some of his early pieces were heard by Diaghilev, who asked him to write the score for *The Firebird*. This was followed by some of the greatest music written specially for the ballet, including *Petrushka*, *Le Sacre du Printemps*, *Les Noces* and *Apollo*, which marked the beginning of his long association with George Balanchine which continued until Stravinsky's death in 1971. The following year Balanchine's New York City Ballet staged a Stravinsky Festival as a tribute. Over a period of eight days, thirty-one works to Stravinsky's music were staged.

Igor Stravinsky.

■ **ANTONY TUDOR** was born in London in 1908. In the early 1930s he was encouraged by Marie Rambert to choreograph for her Ballet Club. His ballets, such as *Lilac Garden*, *Dark Elegies* and *Undertow*, are mostly very serious and moving. He founded his own company in London in 1937, but it could not continue with the outbreak of the Second World War. Tudor and some of his colleagues went to America to help start American Ballet Theater. He created several ballets for that company including *Romeo and Juliet* for Alicia Markova. He became Director of the Royal Swedish Ballet in 1949, but went through a difficult period when he could not choreograph. Then in 1967 he made *Shadowplay* for the Royal Ballet, one of his greatest creations. He returned to work with American Ballet Theater and was a great encouragement to young dancers such as Gelsey Kirkland. He died in a Buddhist retreat in New York in 1987.

■ **AGRIPPINA VAGANOVA**, who was born in 1879, was a ballerina in the Imperial Theatre in St Petersburg. When the Russian Revolution came in 1917 there was strong opposition to ballet from the Bolsheviks. Vaganova had retired from dancing by this time, but had become interested in teaching. She put her teaching methods into practice first in private schools and then at the Petrograd State Choreographic School, where she trained many of the great twentieth-century Russian ballerinas. Her teachings were written down and form the basis of many ballet classes today: her work and the classes that she gave are a direct link with the classical ballet of pre-Revolution Russia. The school was renamed after her.

■ **EDWARD VILLELLA**, who was born in 1937, danced leading roles with the New York City Ballet almost as soon as he joined the company in 1957. His athletic style of dancing in ballets such as *The Prodigal Son*, together with his engaging personality, helped make dancing an acceptable profession for boys in America.

■ **DAVID WALL** was one of the few dancers to combine a true talent for classical ballet with a real talent for acting. He was born in London in 1946, trained at the Royal Ballet School and joined the Royal Ballet touring company when he graduated in 1963. He joined the main company in 1972 and was one of its most popular stars until he retired to become principal of the Royal Academy of Dancing. He created the roles of Lescaut in Kenneth MacMillan's *Manon* and Crown-Prince Rudolf in *Mayerling*.

GLOSSARY
What's What in Dance

■ **Arabesque**   a pose on one leg with the other extended fully, the body slightly tilted, the arms outstretched and following the line of the body

■ **Attitude**   a pose on one leg with the other raised to a 90-degree angle behind (or in front) of the body, with the knee bent and the thigh parallel to the floor

■ **Ballabile**   dances by the corps de ballet, as in Act One of *Napoli* or the Sylphs' dance in *La Sylphide*

■ **Battements**   the beating steps

■ **Black Bottom**   a dance strongly influenced by African dances, first appearing on Broadway in 1926, causing a scandal because of its bottom-wiggling movements

■ **Bolero**   a Spanish dance in 3/4 time dating from the Middle Ages, but which is best-known through Maurice Ravel's music and Torvill and Dean's ice dancing

■ **Bop**   American dance from the 1950s, done by one person on the spot. Rock music developed out of it

■ **Bossa Nova**   a mixture of jazz and the South American samba

■ **Bourrée**   a sixteenth-century French folk dance which was danced by peasant women in clogs; *also* small steps on pointe which give the effect of gliding across the stage, used, for example, for the entry of the Queen of the Wilis in *Giselle*

■ **Cakewalk**   originally performed by black Americans in competition for a cake, it became a jaunty, strutting dance at the beginning of the century

■ **Cancan** a music-hall dance with high kicks, splits and skirt-lifting, which was most popular towards the end of the last century

■ **Cha-cha** a Cuban dance which became popular in the 1950s

■ **Changements** jumps during which the feet cross in the air

■ **Charleston** a social dance that came from Charleston, South Carolina, USA, where black dock-workers made it up to amuse themselves. Brought to Broadway in the Ziegfeld Follies and loved by the 'flappers' of the 1920s

■ **Czardas** folk dance from Hungary, starting slow and then becoming very fast

■ **Danseur noble** princely male dancer

■ **Dedans** inwards, as in *pirouettes en dedans*

■ **Demi-pointe** on half-point, standing on the ball of the foot

■ **Enchainement** a sequence of steps that build up into a 'chain' of movement, becoming a short dance

■ **Épaulement** the placing of the shoulders in relation to the body, which in turn affects the way the head is held

■ **Flamenco** a Spanish dance of great passion, with heel-stamping accompanied by castanet playing

■ **Fouetté** the fast whipping turns seen, for example, in the Black Swan *pas de deux* in *Swan Lake*

■ **Foxtrot** ragtime dance started by Harry Fox, a band-leader. Now performed more elegantly in ballroom dancing

■ **Grand battement** high kicks

■ **Grand jeté** the big jump, making an arc across the stage

■ **Grand plié** deep knee-bends performed at the beginning of class

■ **Hornpipe** a sailors' dance to a wind instrument, stylized as a stage dance

■ **Jitterbug** an energetic dance (also called the lindy) in which one dancer swings another in the air after athletic double work

■ **Jive** a quieter version of the jitterbug, in which dancers were able to make up many of their own steps

■ **Leotard** a one-piece costume used by dancers, invented by Jules Léotard, a French trapeze-artist in the middle of the nineteenth century

■ **Mamba** a Cuban dance mixing Latin American and jazz rhythms. On one beat a step is missed out

■ **Mazurka** a Polish round dance for four or eight couples, the steps including the characteristic heel-tapping

■ **Pas** a step, as in *pas de deux*, *pas de chat*, etc.

■ **Pirouette** a turn on one leg on half or full pointe

■ **Polka** a dance from Bohemia (now part of Czechoslovakia) with a catchy 2/4 time which became equally popular on stage and in the ballroom

■ **Polonaise** a stately court dance from Poland

■ **Port de bras** the positions of the arms and the way they are held

■ **Repertoire** the lists of ballets a company performs most regularly

■ **Révérence** the bow or curtsy after class or performance

■ **Rosin** a substance which comes from turpentine which dancers use, in powder form, to rub on the soles of their shoes before dancing, to avoid slipping

■ **Rumba** an erotic dance from Cuba, mixing African and Caribbean rhythms

■ **St Vitus' Dance** an illness, not a dance, which was common in the fourteenth century; thought to come from eating poisonous fungus which made sufferers jump about in frenzy

■ **Samba**   a Brazilian dance copied from the dances of the first slaves, taken to America in 1939

■ **Square dance**   an American country-dance in which couples face each other in square formations and change places with each other according to instructions from the 'caller'

■ **Tango**   a dance from Argentina, in 2/4 time, which became very popular in Europe and America in the early years of this century

■ **Tour en l'air**   a jump with a turn or turns in the air, usually performed by a male dancer

■ **Travesti**   when dancers appear as members of the opposite sex. Franz in the original production of *Coppélia* in 1870 was danced by a girl, and Frederick Ashton and Robert Helpmann created the roles of the Ugly Sisters in Ashton's *Cinderella*

■ **Turn-out**   the turning out of the legs at the hip-joints to enable the legs to be at right-angles to the body

■ **Tutu**   the ballerina's skirt, which in the Romantic era came to mid-calf with a bell-shaped skirt and a tight bodice, but which was shortened by classical ballerinas at the end of the nineteenth century to show off their virtuoso leg movements

■ **Waltz**   a dance for a couple, in 3/4 time, which originated in Germany and was criticized in the early nineteenth century as the man and woman had to hold each other very close to revolve around the dance floor

■ DANCES IN TIME

■ PREHISTORIC
Fertility dances, war dances

■ CLASSICAL AGE
Bacchic dances, Morris dances

■ MIDDLE AGES
Basse Danse, Bransle, May dances

■ 15TH CENTURY
Hornpipe, Moresque

■ 16TH CENTURY
Allemande, Bourrée, Chaconne, Galliard, Pavane, Saraband, Sir Roger de Coverly, La Volta (Queen Elizabeth I's favourite dance)

■ 17TH CENTURY
Flamenco, Gavotte, Jig

■ 18TH CENTURY
Cotillon, Minuet

■ 19TH CENTURY
Early: Bolero, Galop, Lancers, Mazurka, Polka, Polonaise, Quadrille, Waltz
Late: Barn Dance, Cakewalk, Cancan, Square Dance

■ 1900–1920

Bunny Hug, Tango, Turkey Trot, Veleta, Foxtrot, Lindy Hop

■ 1920–1940

Black Bottom, Charleston, Quickstep, Rumba, Conga, Jitterbug, Lambeth Walk, Palais Glide, Paso Doble, Samba

■ 1940–1960

Jitterbug, Bop, Cha-cha, Jive, Twist

■ 1960–198?

Bossa Nova, Frug, Hully-Gully, Jerk, Shake, Hustle, Salsa, Disco, Break

■TIME CHARTS OF DANCE

Here are some of the most important dates in ballet history, together with dates of historic events, to give you an idea of what was happening in the world.

1581 The *Ballet Comique de la Reine* performed

1603 Queen Elizabeth I dies

1606 Guy Fawkes executed for his part in the Gunpowder Plot

1607 Monteverdi's opera *Orfeo* produced, the first opera to include ballet scenes

1620 The Pilgrim Fathers land in America

1653 Louis XIV dances the role of the *Sun King*

1661 Louis XIV founds the Royal Academy of Dance

1696 Peter the Great becomes Tsar of Russia

1700 Beauchamp writes down the five positions of the feet in ballet

1735 Anne, Empress of Russia, opens the Imperial State Ballet School in St Petersburg

1748 The Royal Danish Theatre opens in Copenhagen

1760 Noverre begins work on his *Lettres*, which change ballet into a theatrical art

1770 Captain Cook discovers Australia

1776 American Declaration of Independence signed

1789 The French Revolution starts

1789 Dauberval's *La Fille Mal Gardée* danced for the first time

1792 John Durang, the first professional American dancer, appears in New York

1804 Richard Trevithick builds the first steam locomotive

1810 Jules Perrot, creator of *Giselle*, is born

1815 Wellington defeats Napoleon at the Battle of Waterloo

1820 Carlo Blasis's *Elementary Treatise upon the Theory and Practice of the Art of Dancing* published

1822 The first print showing a ballerina on pointe is made; in Paris, gaslight first used

1826 Niepce takes the first-ever photograph

1832 Marie Taglioni dances the première of *La Sylphide*

1834 *La Sylphide* danced for the first time in America

1835 Samuel Morse makes the first telegraph machine

1836 Auguste Bournonville, ballet master in Copenhagen, stages his version of *La Sylphide*

1837 Queen Victoria comes to the throne of Britain

1839 The first American *danseur noble*, George Washington Smith, makes his debut

1841 The first performance of *Giselle*

1845 Taglioni, Cerrito, Grahn and Grisi dance the *Pas de Quatre* in London

1846 Thousands die in Ireland when the potato crops fail

1846 *Giselle* staged in America for the first time

1847 Marius Petipa goes to St Petersburg as principal dancer

1860 The Maryinsky Theatre opens in St Petersburg

1861 The American Civil War begins

1865 Abraham Lincoln assassinated on Good Friday

1870 Saint-Léon's *Coppélia* premièred in Paris

1877 *Swan Lake* first performed, in Moscow. It is a failure

1885 Italian dancer Virginia Zucchi dazzles Russian audiences

1885 **Karl Benz builds an engine and instals it in his first car**

1890 Petipa's *The Sleeping Beauty* first performed

1892 Petipa and Ivanov's *The Nutcracker* first performed

1893 Tchaikovsky dies

1895 Petipa and Ivanov's version of *Swan Lake* first produced

1899 **The Boer War starts in South Africa**

1899 Pavlova makes her debut at the Maryinsky Theatre; Isadora Duncan gives her first recital

1901 **Marconi sends the first radio signals across the Atlantic**

1903 **The Wright Brothers make the first flight in a powered heavier-than-air machine**

1904 George Balanchine born in St Petersburg; Frederick Ashton is born in Guayaquil, Ecuador

1907 Fokine creates *The Dying Swan* for Pavlova

1908 **Henry Ford produces the first Model-T Ford**

1909 Fokine's *Les Sylphides* performed in Paris

1910 London sees *Swan Lake* for the first time; *The Firebird* is premiered in Paris

1912 Nijinsky choreographs *L'Après-midi d'un Faune*

1912 **The *Titanic* sinks**

1914 **Outbreak of World War I**

1917 **The Russian Revolution**

1920 The Royal Academy of Dancing is founded in Britain

1924 George Balanchine becomes choreographer to the Ballets Russes

1926 Martha Graham gives her first solo recital; in London, Frederick Ashton's first choreography is danced in a revue; de Valois founds her Academy of Choreographic Art

1928 Balanchine creates *Apollo*

1928 **Women get the vote in Britain**

1929 The last performance of Diaghilev's Ballets Russes

1929 **The Wall Street Crash: the beginning of the Great Depression**

1931 Anna Pavlova dies; the Vic-Wells Ballet gives its first performance

1933 **Hitler comes to power in Germany**

1933 Balanchine leaves for America and founds the School of American Ballet

1934 Alicia Markova dances *Giselle* in the first all-English production

1935 First performance by the School of American Ballet

1939 The Second World War starts

1939 Royal Winnipeg Ballet formed

1940 American Ballet Theater's first New York season

1941 The Japanese attack Pearl Harbor

1942 Fokine dies

1944 American Ballet Theater première *Fancy Free*

1945 Atomic bombs are dropped on Hiroshima and Nagasaki

1946 Margot Fonteyn dances in *The Sleeping Beauty* with the Sadler's Wells Ballet to mark the re-opening of The Royal Opera House, Covent Garden

1948 New York City Ballet gives its first performance; in London, Ashton's *Cinderella*, the first full-length English ballet, is premièred

1950 The Korean War starts

1950 Nijinsky dies in London; Festival Ballet has first London season

1951 The National Ballet of Canada is founded

1952 Queen Elizabeth II comes to the British throne

1956 The Bolshoi Ballet makes its first tour of the West

1961 Yuri Gagarin becomes the first man in space

1961 Rudolf Nureyev 'leaps for freedom' at Paris Airport

These two great events of world and ballet history marked the arrival of the space age and a new era in ballet. Nureyev's defection from Russia helped improve the quality of male dancing in the West. His legendary partnership with Margot Fonteyn took her dancing to new heights and brought a new public to ballet. With Ballet Rambert becoming a modern dance company in 1966 and the founding of the London Contemporary Dance Theatre in 1969 (the year Neil Armstrong walked on the moon) a new young audience in Britain discovered modern dance.